Lesbians Over 60
Speak for Themselves

The *Research on Homosexuality* series:

Series Editor: John P. De Cecco, PhD, Director, Center for Research and Education in Sexuality, San Francisco State University, and Editor, *Journal of Homosexuality*.

Homosexuality and the Law, edited by Donald C. Knutson, JD

Historical Perspectives on Homosexuality, edited by Sal Licata, PhD, and Robert P. Petersen, PhD candidate.

Nature and Causes of Homosexuality: A Philosophic and Scientific Inquiry, edited by Noretta Koertge, PhD

Homosexuality & Psychotherapy: A Practitioner's Handbook of Affirmative Models, edited by John C. Gonsiorek, PhD

Alcoholism & Homosexuality, edited by Thomas O. Zeibold, PhD, and John Mongeon

Literary Visions of Homosexuality, edited by Stuart Kellogg

Homosexuality and Social Sex Roles, edited by Michael W. Ross, PhD

Bisexual and Homosexual Identities: Critical Theoretical Issues, edited by John P. De Cecco, PhD, and Michael G. Shively, MA

Bisexual and Homosexual Identities: Critical Clinical Issues, edited by John P. De Cecco, PhD

Homophobia: An Overview, edited by John P. De Cecco, PhD

Bisexualities: Theory and Research, edited by Fritz Klein, MD, and Timothy J. Wolf, PhD

Anthropology and Homosexual Behavior, edited by Evelyn Blackwood, PhD (cand.)

Historical, Literary, and Erotic Aspects of Lesbianism, edited by Monika Kehoe, PhD

Interdisciplinary Research on Homosexuality in the Netherlands, edited by A. X. van Naerssen

Psychotherapy with Homosexual Men and Women: Integrated Identity Approaches for Clinical Practice, edited by Eli Coleman, PhD

Psychopathology and Psychotherapy in Homosexuality, edited by Michael Ross, PhD

The Pursuit of Sodomy: Male Homosexuality in Renaissance and Enlightenment Europe, edited by Kent Gerard and Gert Hekma

Lesbians Over 60 Speak for Themselves, edited by Monika Kehoe

This series is published by The Haworth Press, Inc., under the editorial auspices of the Center for Research and Education in Sexuality, San Francisco State University, and the *Journal of Homosexuality*.

Lesbians Over 60 Speak for Themselves

Monika Kehoe, PhD

The Haworth Press
New York • London

Lesbians Over 60 Speak for Themselves has also been published as the *Journal of Homosexuality*, Volume 16, Numbers 3/4 1988.

The Haworth Press, Inc., 12 West 32 Street, New York, NY 10001
EUROSPAN/Haworth, 3 Henrietta Street, London WC2E 8LU England

LIBRARY OF CONGRESS
Library of Congress Cataloging-in-Publication Data

Kehoe, Monika.
    Lesbians over 60 speak for themselves / [compiled by] Monika Kehoe.
       p. cm.
    Also published as a special volume issue of the Journal of homosexuality, v. 16, no. 3/4, 1989.
    Includes bibliographical references.
    ISBN 0-86656-816-6
    1. Aged lesbians—United States. I. Title. II. Title: Lesbians over sixty speak for them-selves.
HQ75.6.U5K44 1988b
306.7'66'0880565—dc19   88-24304
                                                           CIP

Lesbians Over 60
Speak for Themselves

CONTENTS

Introduction	**1**
Chapter 1: The Project	**3**
History	3
Purpose	4
Method	4
The Questionnaire	4
Research Limitations	6
Research Prior to 1980	7
The Future of Elder-Lesbian Research	8
Chapter 2: The Background (1900-1950)	**11**
Growing Up	12
Careers	13
Butch/Femme Roles	16
Gay Bars	18
Lesbians in the Military	19
Closeted and Surviving	21
Coming Out	25
A Personal Note	27
Chapter 3: Family and Other Social Relationships	**29**
With Parents and Siblings	29
With Children	30
With Husbands	31
With Other Men and Women	32
Senior Centers	34
Informal Gatherings	34
Lesbian and Gay Organizations for Seniors	36
Loneliness and Isolation	36

Age Mates   39
Retirement   39
Community Living   40
Life Satisfaction   41

Chapter 4: Lesbian Relationships and Homosexuality   43

Before and After 60   44
Lesbian Identity and Sex   46
Bisexuality   47
Couples   48

Chapter 5: The Present: Growing Old (1950-1980)   53

Physical Health   54
Ill Health and Dependency   56
Emotional Health   57
Attitudes Toward Lesbianism and Aging   60

Chapter 6: Lesbians and Gay Men Over 60   63

Difficulties of Comparison: The Berger and Kehoe Studies   63
Difference in Method   64
Difference in Subjects' Living Situations   66
Difference in Marital Status   67
Difference in Educational Background   67
Difference in Incomes   68
Difference in Psychological and Social Adaptation   68

Conclusion: A Profile of the 60-Plus Lesbian of This Study   75

Summary   76

Appendix   79

Description of Course on "Lesbian and Gay Aging"   79
Evaluation Report   80
Preliminary Report   82
Questionnaire   93

ABOUT THE AUTHOR

Monika Kehoe, PhD, is currently teaching "Lesbian and Gay Aging" in the Gerontology Program at San Francisco State University, where she is also Research Associate in the Center for Research and Education in Sexuality and a member of the Editorial Board of the *Journal of Homosexuality*. She has served as Consultant to the American Society on Aging project on "Lifestyle Planning for the Third Age."

Lesbians Over 60 Speak for Themselves

Introduction

It was not until the early 1970s that serious interest in the subject of women and their relationships to other women was fully ratified by feminist scholarship. Since then, women whose primary relationship is with other women has also become a topic of academic concern.[1] The same decade saw an accelerated increase in gerontological literature and in awareness of the problems of the aged as senior power itself burgeoned. These developments pointed to the previously neglected area of investigation undertaken in this work; namely, data on lesbians over 60. Because age and gender have combined to limit research on sex after 60, even for the general population, one can easily imagine that norms for the behavior of elderly deviant females have not been clearly defined.

Yet lesbianism includes much more than sexual practice, and little is known about the total nature of this deeply hidden group of older women. For many nongays, lesbianism has all the fascination of the mysterious: Who are they? What do they do? And, especially, how did they get that way? However, these questions are seldom applied to *old* lesbians. The preoccupation with youth in our culture underscores the presumption that these elders have died or been converted in their maturity to heterosexualism. Most manuals,[2] which purport to be guides for women to age gracefully, never mention relationships with other women (sexual or otherwise) as a possible solution for the ubiquitous "friendless widow." And yet, for many of the women in the study reported on here, lesbianism is not primarily a sexual relationship at all, but a much wider female interdependence with broader human satisfactions that transcend mere physical attachment.

In the following pages, you will read about this necessarily covert company of women surviving in a hostile society: where they live, how they feel about being "different," how they cope with the homophobia that surrounds them, what they did before they retired (if they have), their present economic and social status, their most pressing problems, and their physical and emotional health, as well as that most intriguing topic, their sexual behavior — as it was in their youth, and as it is now. This you will have in their own words as they responded to the questionnaire they received at their request. *Lesbians Over 60 Speak for Themselves* is not a sociological treatise, nor does it pretend to be a document of flawless scientific research. It is, rather, a pioneer effort to find out about a deeply hidden segment of our population.

NOTES

1. See the first lesbian issue of the *Journal of Homosexuality*, issue *12*(3/4), May 1986, guest edited by the author, and the lesbian issue, *Signs*, 1985, University of Chicago Press.

2. For example, Troll, L. E., Israel, J., & Israel, K. (Eds.). (1977). *Looking ahead: A woman's guide to the problems and joys of growing older*. Englewood Cliffs, NJ: Prentice-Hall.

Chapter 1

The Project

HISTORY

The 60-plus lesbian research project of 1984 reported on here was preceded by a nationwide study of 50 lesbians over 65 begun part-time in 1980 under the auspices of the Americas Behavioral Research Corporation in San Francisco.[1] In April of 1982, I was able to transfer the project to the Center for Research and Education in Sexuality (CERES) at San Francisco State University, where as a research associate I could work on it full-time. Three months later, in July of 1982, I was joined by research assistant Sheryl Goldberg. We completed the preliminary study of lesbians over 65 in November of 1983.

For this initial inquiry, we had no budget or salary, other than $100 for postage. What we did have was a base of operation at CERES, where facilities and equipment were generously shared with us in anticipation of the grant we had applied for to expand the study. We also had dedicated volunteer graduate-student help, and the first questionnaire was printed through the courtesy of the San Francisco State University Students' Women's Center.[2] At the end of 1983, we received support from the Chicago Resources Center ($22,148) and San Francisco's Golden Gate Business Association ($500). This allowed us three additional salaried personnel: an evaluator, a word processor, and a computer programmer, along with additional work-study student assistants. We were also able to double (to 100) the number of subjects and to afford a new, professionally printed questionnaire. We decided to drop the minimum age level from 65 to 60 in order to widen the scope of subject recruitment.

PURPOSE

The new project was to gather information on a hidden population that had never before been investigated exclusively in this age group, in order to secure a needs assessment, and to disseminate the findings as widely as possible. Doing so could (a) help reduce homophobia, (b) sensitize those who work with the aged, and (c) support the establishment of retirement facilities for lesbians.

METHOD

The greatest difficulty in any attempt to survey a hidden population is, of course, to find respondents willing to talk about themselves. The question, then, is how to reach them, how to get them to cooperate. An anonymous questionnaire seemed the least intrusive means, but in order to distribute it, addresses were necessary. Because there was at that time no organization for old lesbians, we began by placing announcements in lesbian/feminist newsletters and periodicals, sending posters to feminist bookstores and women's centers, and writing letters to directors of Women's Studies programs at colleges and universities, as well as to the gay caucuses of academic associations. These announcements described the project and asked those eligible to write or call if they were willing to participate.

THE QUESTIONNAIRE

An introductory letter appeared on the back of the cover to the 26-page brochure (see Appendix), while the back page invited additional comments. The instrument was pretested on a dozen eligible participants, and additional copies were given to professional colleagues for suggested revisions. The final version, containing 87 items (in large print) was titled, "Lesbians-Over-60: A National Survey for Older Women Whose Emotional and/or Sexual Preferences Are for Other Women." The survey took about 40 minutes to complete. Many returned questionnaires had additional pages attached or lengthy comments in the margins.

The 87 items covered were numbered under the following 8

headings: Life-Style Identification, Social Life, Services for Older Adults, Family Relationships, Relationships with Other Women, Sexuality, Health, and Background Information. The section titles indicate what kind of information we hoped to gather. First, we tried to find out how lesbians of the 60-plus generation feel about being labeled deviant and what terminology, if any, they preferred in reference to themselves. Second, we wanted to learn how they spend their free time and what connections they have, if any, to the wider gay community. In order to establish the need for gay senior centers, separate from those provided for the general public, we asked to what extent they use mainline senior services. In connection with these queries, we tried to discover which of the problems facing the elderly were the most severe for our participants. Under "Family Relationships," we wanted to accumulate as much data as possible, not only on kind and number of relatives and marital history, but on attitudes between nongay family members and respondents regarding their different life-styles.

In the section "Relationships with Other Women," we defined *relationship* as "having both emotional and physical/sexual components," in an effort to minimize possible confusion or misinterpretation. We attempted to ascertain the age at which our subjects first recognized their same-gender attraction and, in a separate question, the age when they actually had their first relationship with another woman. Were they currently involved, and if so for how long? Did they prefer younger or older women? What roles, if any, did they play? Among the questions in this section, those relating to the aftermath of the death of a partner elicited the most revealing responses.

The section on "Sexuality" gave us an opportunity to inquire into the attitudes and behavior of our respondents, in this most concealed part of their lives, and how these have changed as they age. We wanted some facts on the prevalence of celibacy. Does sex become less important among the elderly in the lesbian community, and is this by choice or because of lack of opportunity?

Although the section on "Health" may not have presented the possibility of similarly intriguing questions, we did need to know the physical, mental, and emotional condition of our subjects, including their use of alcohol and other drugs. Besides questions on these topics, we attached a life-satisfaction scale[3] and several questions on discrimination to conclude this section. In the final "Background" section, we collected demographic information and the present status (financial, religious, and political affiliation) of our participants.

Out of 134 questionnaires sent out at the request of those willing to participate in our project (or someone who knew someone eligible who might be willing to answer), 106 were returned, all within a 4-month period. We used the first 100 received.

RESEARCH LIMITATIONS

The principal weakness of this research data is, therefore, fairly clear. It has not reached a cross-section of the population it attempts to investigate. Because "we are everywhere," as lesbians are fond of announcing, there are all of those in the 60-plus age group (an estimated 1.8 million[4]) who are still deeply closeted and unwilling to come out and be scrutinized. There are those within the ethnic minorities, some of whom remain silent for reasons of family or religion. There are those less educated, less secure, less articulate — who do not frequent bookstores, subscribe to feminist/lesbian newsletters or periodicals, or participate in college or women-center activities — who do not trust academics snooping into their lives, even if they hear about an enterprise such as ours. Then there are those who "abhor labels" or do not identify as lesbians. In short, our means of recruitment, the so-called "snowball" technique, almost ensured that our participants would be literate, articulate caucasians, above average in health, education, and income. But how to reach the others in the 60-plus category when they do not frequent bars or even those few metropolitan organizations such as SAGE (Senior Action in a Gay Environment) in New York City or GLOE (Gay and Lesbian Outreach to Elders) in San Francisco that cater to senior gays?

Besides recruitment inadequacies, other limitations were disclosed in the course of the study. Some were called to our attention by the respondents themselves who mentioned, for example, our neglect of detailed inquiries regarding hearing impairment,[5] "a very isolating form of physical deterioration associated with aging," as one wrote. We regret not including a question on pets and their influence on life satisfaction, particularly of those elderly women who live alone.[6] The ambiguity and potential misinterpretation of some of the terms used in the questionnaire were also made clear by the confusion expressed in the answers; for example, to Question No. 39, "Do you feel that being a lesbian is your choice?" which inadvertently raised the old etiological bugaboo of homosexuality.

RESEARCH PRIOR TO 1980

Several pioneer efforts have been made since the late 1970s to unmask this covert company of "older" women. The problem of finding them has always been the severest handicap. "Older" or "aging" are relative terms, depending on one's perspective, which changes as one advances in years. In the lesbian and gay community, the words generally refer to anyone over 40. However, several studies have included lesbians over 60:

1. Minnegerode and Adelman investigated the adaptations and problems of 5 lesbians and 6 gay men, 66 to 77 years of age, in a study at San Francisco State University in 1978.
2. Twenty West Coast lesbians over 50 years old were interviewed by Minna Robinson for her master's thesis at California State University, Dominguez Hills, in 1979. Included were 7 subjects over the age of 60.
3. Twenty-five lesbians over 60 were studied for a master's thesis prepared by Chris Almvig and published by Utica College Press, New York, in 1982.
4. Finally, my own 65-plus survey of 50 lesbians was completed at San Francisco State University in 1983.[7]

This rather sparse preliminary research suggests the difficulty experienced by those who have attempted to describe this advanced age group of gay women. As Raymond Berger admitted in the introduction to his excellent book, *Gay and Gray*,[8] in which he recorded interviews with 7 male homosexuals and reported on questionnaire responses from 112 gay men over 40:

The older women are simply less accessible to the probing eye of the researcher. As Chapter 9 (p. 121) explains, we were unable to collect sufficient data on the older lesbian and therefore decided to limit *Gay and Gray* to males. (p. 13)

Although he said he made "special appeals for help in locating minority and female respondents," he was successful in securing interviews with only "eight women and questionnaires from eighteen" (p. 125). He did not specify how old they were. However, because his cut-off age was 40, they may have been less than 60.[9] In view of the difficulties in finding subjects in the 60-plus age range at all, we felt fortunate to have been able to reach more than 100. We continued to receive letters throughout 1985 from additional eligible participants expressing a willingness to complete our questionnaire. In each case, we replied that we had collected the necessary number and requested permission to keep the name of the writer on file for possible later contact.

THE FUTURE OF ELDER-LESBIAN RESEARCH

I used to agree, at least tacitly, with the premise that the job of the lesbian/gay researcher was to establish that homosexuals are just like heterosexuals and just as respectable. I even looked forward to assembling 100 "matching" heterosexual women over 60 for a comparative study with the lesbians already investigated. Yet recently, I have been persuaded that such a comparison only continues to polarize the old homo/hetero dichotomy in which we, as the minority, are trying to prove our probity. Now, I would hope, along with Katz,[10] for the expansion of a new frontier:

To the extent that homosexual and heterosexual represent a limiting imposition on humanity, a labeling created for the purpose, and functioning in the interest of social control, we should consider how to transcend that polarity in theory and practice. . . . There exists today a pressing personal need for us to reclaim that which is life-enhancing and lovely within the "lesbian" and "gay" community. Yet we have, I think, a simultaneous need to dive down deep, to risk, to question, to continually challenge the old terms, assumptions, and institutions, to radically remake the meaning of our lives and restructure the social organization of our bodies. (p. 173)

In the process of renaming and remaking, we may want to look for models of the durability that remains desirable in both homosexual and heterosexual relationships. To this end, more couples research focused on lesbian elders in the 60-plus age group might help us understand what elements have contributed to the longevity of those relationships; for example, those that have lasted more than 2 decades.[11] The impact of feminism on these long-term lesbian dyads is another area of inquiry that would be of considerable historical interest.

Of course, the greatest need in all research on homosexuals is to broaden the scope of sampling to include ethnic minorities and other categories not presently represented in published studies. With more funding, we should find it possible to do more in-depth interviewing and thus avoid the misinterpretations inherently possible in mailed questionnaires. As more elders come out of the closet in a more tolerant society, and new ways are devised to reach them, we should be able to come up with models of a satisfactory alternative lifestyle that would be a boon to all of those who otherwise might succumb to loneliness, the number one problem of the aging woman in America.

NOTES

1. For prior studies of "older" lesbians, see later in this chapter.

2. For my report on this research, see *Journal of Homosexuality*, *12*(3/4), May 1986.

3. Index A developed by Neugarten, Havighurst, and Tobin (1961), modified by Adams (1969) and Wood et al. (1969).

4. A figure based on the 1980 U.S. Census total of women over 60 adjusted according to Kinsey's (1953) conservative estimate of 8% as homosexual.

5. This was an issue only touched on in Question No. 48.

6. For more on the subject of animal assisted therapy, see my forthcoming article in the *Journal of Homosexuality*, entitled "Loneliness and the Aging Homosexual."

7. For a report on this survey, see my article in the *Journal of Homosexuality*, *12*(3/4), May 1986, which I edited and which was also published separately

under the title *Historical, Literary and Erotic Aspects of Lesbianism*, New York: Harrington Park Press, 1986.

8. Berger, R. (1982). *Gay and gray*. Urbana, IL: University of Illinois Press.

9. For a comparison of the Berger and Kehoe studies, see Chapter 6.

10. Katz, J. N. (1983). *Gay/lesbian almanac: A new documentary*. New York: Harper & Row.

11. For a concise overview of research on homosexual couples of both sexes, see Peplau, L. A. (1982). Research on homosexual couples: An overview. *Journal of Homosexuality*, *8*(2), 3-8.

Chapter 2

The Background
(1900-1950)

The fields of scientific study dealing with human development biology, psychology, and sociology — all come together in gerontology to focus on older people. The physical conditions that exist among those in this age group are well known: failing senses, declining physical resiliency, decreasing muscular strength, circulatory problems, and deterioration of organs and bodily systems, including loss of ability to withstand disease. The combination of all these is known as senescence.

Along with these physical symptoms come psychological changes such as decline in memory, in psychomotor performance and in sensory acuity. Social factors seem to be as important as biological in the psychology of aging. One of the most important for the person living alone is isolation and its consequent loneliness. Women, as survivors, experience this more than men. Everyone is aware that girls are socialized differently from boys. As adults they have different roles, different expectations and experiences. Society reacts to them differently and they develop adequate social functioning in different ways. However, every individual's social situation changes with growing old, and this alteration affects attitudes, values, and beliefs so that, besides the differences between men and women, obvious differences develop in attitudes, values, and beliefs held by the young and the old — a subject we will comment on later.

Our concern here is specifically with older lesbians, many of whom, although having experienced the same or comparable physical and psychological changes, have not always had the same life course or role conversions as their nongay sisters. Nor has there been a particular schedule mandated for them to conform to in their subculture. On the other hand, widowhood, retirement, dependency, and illness may have altered their situation along with that of other women in later life. For example, one respondent who checked loneliness as her most serious problem has experienced the lesbian equivalent of widowhood: "My roommate for almost half our lives died in 1981 and I have been alone since then."

GROWING UP

The kind of social environment that American lesbians born in the early part of the century lived in would have been an important influence on their growing up, as well as now that they are senior citizens. The majority of those we surveyed were reared in towns or cities in all regions of the continental U.S. Almost a fourth spent their childhood in rural areas, while a fifth said they had lived as children in suburbia. Five were born outside the country. One identifies herself as American Indian and another as black, two as Asians, and all the rest as white. No Hispanic women responded.

Their religious upbringing included 13 Catholic, 12 Jewish, and 29 Protestant. One is Buddhist, while 15 checked "other." The remainder indicated no religious affiliation. Some, along with many of those in the general population, "belong" primarily for social reasons. In answer to our question (No. 77), "How frequently do you attend religious or spiritual services?" one noted, "I attend Unitarian activities (women's group, camping, dancing) but seldom the services."

Their educational background was above average: all completed high school; 16 added two years of college; one-fifth earned a bachelor's degree, while almost half attended graduate school with 21 receiving advanced degrees. Twenty-two were still following courses in continuing education at the time of the questionnaire (1984) or working on their first degree. A self-employed sexagenarian commented on the difficulty (one which any woman might encounter) she had had in her attempt to complete her professional education:

I had only a small amount of work to do to finish my doctorate — went to the university in my late 40s and I was told that the first choice for candidates was young men, next older males, next young women and last older women, regardless of their record because that was the order in which they were hired.

CAREERS

In spite of such discrimination — and other more specific to their lifestyle — 73 had had professional careers and several had been university instructors. Many were caregivers, while others had been educational administrators, elementary or high school teachers, research scientists, or artists. Some worked in civil service, a few (previously married) designated themselves as "mother" or "homemaker." Ten were involved in industrial or business enterprises, and some had had more than one career. Eight checked "clerical," four "trades," three "domestic." One simply said she had managed her ranch. Although there were a few who had been librarians or physical education instructors, the results of the questionnaire did not support the P.E.-nurse-librarian expectation of lesbian occupations. Thirty-two of the hundred respondents are still working full- or part-time, while 60 are retired and eight consider themselves unemployed. Seventy-two made comments regarding discrimination in their work life, and one attributed it at least in part to her appearance: "In employment I have found a distinct antagonism from management and co-workers because of my masculinity in appearance." Another self-employed "late bloomer" who had been married and divorced remarked about her colleagues: "I sense that men who are sexually insecure resent women who are independent and assertive. I am uncomfortable in public with butch-like women who give me away. Consequently I steer clear of masculine women." One remembered the anxiety of her military experience in 1952:

The WACS made it impossible for me to stay in service and I always thought it was because of a too rebellious persona but, in looking back, I don't know. Nothing was ever said. Maybe they didn't want to confront that lesbian possibility themselves.

In the same vein, a retired educator reported: "I was fired from teaching in a college — they wouldn't admit this was the reason but I'm sure it was."

The first half of the century, before the onset of the feminist movement, was a time when lesbians were likely to face more severe discrimination in public life as females than as lesbians because they were generally careful to conceal their affectional preference. It was a different America then.

I was born in 1909, but 10% of the respondents to our surveys were born even earlier. What was it like growing up as a lesbian in the first decades of this century? For most it was, at best, awkward and puzzling. Sexuality was never talked about openly, much less homosexuality. The only book we knew about homosexuality among women, *The Well of Loneliness*, was not always easy to get, even in urban areas.[1] Most parents, even if they were readers of such an arcane subject, were less sophisticated than parents today and would have been at a loss to comprehend a daughter's confession of "affectional preference" for girls. Indeed, vocabulary to describe such feelings, other than medically, was unknown.

Then, too, most of us were brought up in the Judeo-Christian tradition, in church-going families, and we learned early about sins against chastity, with only clouded reference to the mortal sin "against nature" that was always cloaked in tantalizing circumlocutions we didn't comprehend. One respondent, reflecting on her childhood, wrote:

I was brought up to go to church and went. I'd take my aunt to church every Sunday. The preacher gave us "Hell's Fire and Damnation" to the point I could not believe a merciful God could cast a body into Hell's fire and burn for eternity. When I became self-supporting, I stopped going to church. When I became aware that there were others like me, and the church damned us, I did not return.

Another reported, "My Catholic upbringing made my life miserable when I discovered I was a lesbian, and for many years I found myself torn between acting on my feelings and the perceived consequences and guilt." One who identifies herself as a Methodist added this P.S.: "My life experience as a lesbian has always been in conflict with my church membership, and the need to lie to the world about the most important part of my life has always been painful."

As we passed through high school and on to college, we learned that "homosexuality," as it was called, was an illness to be cured, a "perversion," or, at best, a "phase" outgrown in adulthood. Like *The Well of Loneliness*, this was all pretty depressing news and required considerable ego satisfaction in other areas of our lives for us to maintain psychological equilibrium. Some young lesbians, in the early decades of the century, went along with the tide and adjusted to a heterosexual marriage. Others fled to the convent.[2] Because there was less opportunity for women to support themselves in pre-World War II America, one may surmise that the convent was sometimes a refuge (as it was in medieval Europe) for women who wished to avoid the social pressures of a conventional male/female marriage.

Likewise, in the first half of this century, there were far fewer opportunities than there are now for women to attain distinction in any field. In sports, an avocation that appealed to many young lesbians then as now, they had little encouragement or reward for achieving excellence. Of course, there were sport stars like Gertrude Ederle or Bebe Didrickson, but they were rare exceptions. The fitness craze had not yet arrived on the American scene to absorb young women's energy and make it possible for them to realize the physical pleasures, other than sexual, that their bodies could give them. If there were women in sports, then, who worked out strenuously enough to alter their menstrual cycle, it was never mentioned, and certainly would never have been construed as a desirable side effect of such activities. There were few professional sports teams for women; it was considered unladylike for them to compete, and who would pay to watch girls running around in bloomers anyway! Their participation in the Olympics was much more restricted than it is today. Strenuous sports were deemed bad for women's health. Body-building was unheard of for them. Females were expected to be "feminine." Parents discouraged little girls from running, playing ball, climbing trees, or doing anything that might make them sweat or dirty their pretty dresses.[3] As they matured, their interest was supposed to turn to boys—not as playmates, but rather as "dates" or marriage prospects. There was to be no gender confusion.

BUTCH/FEMME ROLES

"Lady-like" behavior did not always appeal to those who were lesbians, even though they may not have yet identified themselves as such. Some preferred to do boy's things, play their games: Jacks, tiddly winks, or playing with dolls they found tiresome.[4] Some grew up to choose a butch role in their lesbian relationships, while still retaining some of the tenderness, compassion, sensitivity, nurturance, and other virtues traditionally associated with the feminine gender. They often developed what was later to be described as an androgynous personality, a fashionable topic for psychological inquiry. Others tried to imitate men in all aspects and assumed a "macho" personality.

Although butch/femme role-playing is not supported, or even acknowledged, by most of those surveyed, it should be pointed out that, without any other model, wife/husband roles became a common pattern for lesbian relationships in this early era, particularly for "working-class" lesbians,[5] just as cross-dressing was often the way some women who wanted male privilege (or found corsets, high heels, and petticoats inhibiting) sought to "pass" as men. In answer to the question, "Have their been conventional heterosexual roles played in your relationship?" a respondent who had been married twice to men, checked "yes" and added:

I suppose so, in the sense that I have usually played the typical female role in being the first to indicate my interest—the stage-setter for a sexual union—then the other woman usually takes over and I reciprocate (about the same roles as with men). The day to day relating was pretty equal (as it was with men in my case) although three times I've been attracted to feminine women but couldn't carry it off.

Another, never married to a man, who "dated all through college" and "became informally engaged" to one in her junior year but "never came near having intercourse with a man," wrote this about lesbian roles:

The few relationships I have seen that lasted for many years were monogamous, and each consisted of a dyke and a femme, with everyone knowing who was who. This is not to imply that I think it has to be that way to last, as young lesbians, most of whom do not want to be categorized, may work out a relationship not based on heterosexual marriage.

One woman, also never married, sometimes changed her role: "My friend was active, I passive . . . later I became butch." Another reply specifies role-playing "in first and longest relationship only," one of 22 years. A respondent who had given conventional marriage a 3-month try, admitted:

As I look back, I think I was always a boy in my own mind. My relationships with women were always like a solid marriage—including buying a home, sharing expenses, pets, courting and all the rest.

A rather poignant touch comes through from the perspective of an aging lesbian who noted:

Though I'm supposed to be butch, I never had to pursue or take the initiative when younger. Don't notice anyone chasing after me these days. Guess that good old charisma is gone, alas, like my youth, too soon.

While about a quarter of the women surveyed admitted wanting to change their sex, the majority of those who did specified that it was only in their "early youth" that they entertained such ideas. Although they answered "no" to the question (No. 46), two added comments in the margin: "Always wished I were born a male and hope to be the next time around"; and, "I would have preferred to be a man—many more advantages."

Before the mid-century, the feminist movement had not yet liberated women from the conviction of their own inferiority or given them pride in their womanhood. Nor had fashion discovered unisex or education introduced Women's Studies to open their minds to alternative styles of appearance and female achievement, as well as of woman-to-woman relating. Indeed, we are reminded in *The New Our Bodies, Ourselves*[6] that in the 1980s there has been something of a revival of this often criticized role-playing:

> Although the codes are less strict nowadays, in one way or another many lesbians continue to explore the butch-femme evocation of assertiveness and receptivity, its celebration of "difference in women's textures" and its particular forms of courageous eroticism. (p. 149)

GAY BARS

The hold of custom is strong even in an evolving "democratic" society where the young are especially vulnerable to its grip. The United States was considered a "melting pot" in the early decades of the century, but not for "minorities" deviant from its established behavioral conformity. There was no room for sexual diversity in the vision of the founding fathers, who reflected the Puritan ethic of their origin. Not only were models lacking for lesbians growing up in the first half of this century, but they had little, if any, peer support. There were no "gay" communities for women where they could hope to meet with understanding from other women who shared their difference.

New lesbian bars, where they existed in metropolitan centers in the early 1940s, were in the most undesirable parts of the city and frequently subject to raids by the police vice squads. A woman with a respectable job risked her career by visiting them. Our respondents, mostly retired from "the caring professions" did not, nor would they have dared, look to bars as places for socializing with other lesbians. In spite of the fact that gay bars (usually mixed and under male management) were the only public places they could hope to find understanding company in the "old days," only 7% of those who grew up in urban areas said they had met other lesbians in bars. A 75-year old recalled: "Bars and social-gay lesbian groups were unknown until I joined the Dorians." Deeply closeted in small towns and rural areas, lesbians had little opportunity to socialize with their own kind outside a limited group, and seldom congregated in public places. One from a rural area described their clandestine meetings:

> In the old lesbian world, we met to party—never gave last names nor told where we lived or worked. It was boring but the only way we knew. Most of my old friends are still too fearful to really enjoy life.

LESBIANS IN THE MILITARY

World War II, with its surge toward social change, had its impact on gays as well as on American society at large. Young women with problems of adjustment at home had a chance to escape parental supervision by joining the armed services. Twenty-seven of those answering our questionnaire did. They must have been among the more discreet, though, because only one was discharged because of her lesbianism. As Pat Bond has indicated in the film, "The Word is Out,"[7] staying in military service was a constant challenge for many of the lesbians enrolled in the early days. One of our respondents recalled the "occasional witch hunts to detect lesbians—especially when we were involved in sporting activities" that went on in the Air Force. Another ex-service woman reported: "In the military, harassment by 051 for all who were in sports resulted in many stressful interviews."

Military service, attractive to the young in many ways, was often a troubled period for lesbians. In answer to Question No. 82A,

"Did you receive a discharge because of your lesbianism?" a septuagenarian recollected:

> I was discharged for AWOL of one and a half years, while
> stationed in Europe, and insubordination to a female officer. I
> cursed her! It seemed to me unfair inasmuch as I had been
> through the worst of World War II in the Pacific and the inva-
> sion of the Philippines.

The effects of the rigidity inculcated by years in uniform has
persisted to alter the life of one of our respondents: "My present
partner is a military officer and has had serious problems with her
recent role (3 years) as a lesbian."

Now I, too, a septuagenarian, look back on my years of working
in close collaboration with the military. Although only a civil servant living under USAMGIK (U.S. Military Government in Ko-
rea), I had some quite amusing experiences, such as the time I attended an officer's dance in the Chosen Hotel in Seoul. Just for fun
(I could never resist such opportunities), I thoughtlessly announced,
as I stepped on the dance floor with a congenial male officer, "I
only lead." Fortunately, he was sufficiently inebriated to take this
declaration in stride and we cavorted briefly, ballroom style, with
me trying to push him around. This incident eventually proved to be
important. It was raised some years later when I had my hearing
before the Civil Service Board in New York City. Because of that
encounter years before, I was accused of "moral turpitude." The
penalty for this was a 2-year suspension from the Civil Service.
How did I feel about it then? It bothered me very little because at
the time I was employed by the New York State Department of
Education in Albany and, luckily, worked with a wise and sympathetic director who arranged an assignment for me in New York
City to coincide with my hearing.

In the 1950s, we experienced McCarthyism when Red-baiting
and queer-baiting rounded up "perverts" and lumped them together
with communists as "security risks."[8] Another ex-government em-
ployee described her apprehension during those years: "The constant anxiety of being 'found out' and fired from a job because I

could be blackmailed was terrible. I lived through the McCarthy terror."

It was not until 1955, with the founding of the Daughters of Bilitis (DOB) in San Francisco, that lesbians had an alternative social outlet to the gay bars, which by then had become more dangerous places to frequent for the sake of one's career. In the mid-1950s *The Ladder* began publication, providing for the first time a magazine exclusively for lesbians. It provided information and education that brought awareness and insight to many, especially those on the West and East coasts, where chapters of DOB were being established and moving the organization into an activist middle-class position.

The popular book entitled *Sex After Sixty* begins with the pronouncement, "Every day five thousand Americans turn sixty."[9] We might add, since women outlive men by a substantial margin, "and at least 250 of them are lesbians." In their chapter, "People Without Partners," the authors pointed out that in 1970 more than half of all the women over 60 were widows, as compared to about 15% of men. Their one-paragraph recognition of homosexuality as a viable solution to loneliness, which they mention as the most profound problem of elderly women, is worth quoting here:

> Homosexual unions exist among older people, but little is known about them. Few older homosexual couples have "come out" and revealed their relationship openly, preferring to present themselves as roommates or friends. Homosexuality was not considered an acceptable personal choice when they were younger and they would have been subjected to social censure. Fortunately, this climate is changing. It is our impression that many more older people have chosen homosexuality as a way of life than is commonly realized. (p. 56)

CLOSETED AND SURVIVING

It is certainly not surprising, given the general climate of homophobia of this earlier era, that so many older lesbians were and have remained deeply closeted. A 74-year-old who grew up in a small southern town reflected:

I have no regrets about my long life designation as a lesbian, but did experience years of unhappiness when I had to live in the closet because of it and forced myself to pretend to hetero-sexuality in my social and sexual relationships when within me, emotionally and physically, none existed. That is one of the cruelties of the homosexual's lot in our society, and it represents to me all those miserable years which now in my old age can no longer hurt me — now that it is too late to matter.

The South, with its conservatism and Bible-belt mentality, has always been an area where those who espouse an alternative life-style have experienced condemnation. Another woman with the same background who still lives in the South "alone in a studio apartment" wrote: "It must be wonderful to be able to acknowledge publicly one's love for someone else without shame or censure. It's what I'd most wish for all of us." A third respondent, retired from the Navy, described her present relief in retirement:

While I have always been comfortable with my lesbianism, the emotional strain of leading a double life has been severe. Only in very recent years, since retirement, and living in this unusually tolerant atmosphere that exists in the Bay Area, have I been able to relax somewhat and worry less about what society and my remaining family think of me.

Yet another remembered some of the discomforts of her youth:

I have always been a lesbian; however, when I was young, one definitely was in the Dingy Closet. Having to wear dresses, makeup, etc. was like teaching a left-handed kid to write with the right hand (which, of course, was done). Consequently, this dual personality feeling was a chain dragging behind.

Being closeted, as most lesbians over 60 continue to be even though some may feel more relaxed after retirement, affects them in various ways. One of these, an English woman who answered "yes" to the specific question (No. 26 in the 65-plus study), "Do you consider yourself closeted?" added the following remarks to the subquestion, "If so, what are your apprehensions about admitting your life-style?":

> I do not have "apprehensions." I think (a) it is silly to "come out" when you don't have a lover and may not ever have one; (b) I do not consider my bisexuality as a major element in my life; (c) I like privacy; (d) I find some of the proclaiming publicly one's sexual preference somewhat dubious; (e) I might get involved with a woman who prefers discretion.

In view of the fact that the majority of those who sent back the earlier (65-plus) questionnaire said they were "out of the closet," we did not include that question in the later (60-plus) study. We concluded that our self-identified respondents were, by the very fact of their completing the questionnaire, "uncloseted." However, this has little bearing on the other estimated million-plus lesbians over 60 in the United States. As researchers who have attempted to reach members of this age group have found, they are well hidden. We were fortunate to get replies from 100, even though half of them were the same individuals who had been in our earlier study.

Obviously, the great majority of gays, and especially gay women in the first half of this century (with its pink-triangle mentality), would have kept a very low profile and been extremely cautious not to reveal their affectional preference. Their prudence no doubt continues as they age even in today's more liberal environment; they would be likely to persist in the same dissimulations out of habit, if nothing else. After 7 decades, one stated: "In the eyes of society, it's still an unacceptable lifestyle and I feel myself too vulnerable at this time to 'come out of the closet'."

Given such a background of oppression and clandestine existence, it was almost inevitable that they would be survivors, tough and resilient. Some were undeterred and most have overcome. "At my '55 College Reunion I came out to my classmates and afterwards several tried to avoid me." She was 50 then. At 80, having "come out" at 72, she told us she was in a "loving, nonsexual relationship with a woman and in a sexual relationship with another woman who lives 100 miles away—we spend time together every two or three weeks."

Others have had other more unsettling experiences, but have coped and gone on to stabilize their lives. One respondent in the young-old (65 to 75) age group, a successful entrepreneur with a $50,000-plus annual income, also exemplifies the type who has not resorted to drugs or suicide according to the popular expectations of her day.

> I quite possibly could have been a lesbian prior to my heterosexual marriage. I entered the Air Force on my 18th birthday and had mild lesbian relationships during my 2 years in the military. Got married at the age of 21. After 4 years of marriage discovered my husband to be a transvestite and covert homosexual. We were great companions and compatible mates, but our sexual lives never really jelled. He became an alcoholic and I could in no way have been able to support our four daughters in a manner in which they had been raised. I finally divorced my husband when I felt strong enough to start from the bottom with four teenage daughters. We made it! It was rough but we grew together in love and respect. When my youngest left home, I "came out" and have been a lesbian for 14 years.

Another, an Ivy League college graduate married to a minister, stays closeted for many reasons:

> I'm a therapist so perhaps I know a bit more about myself than the average 70-year-old. I've had more need to know because of my counseling of others. I must admit that I'm still defensive about never having come out, still living with a husband who would, in many ways, be better off without me. There is a 42-year history of this condition. I was in a half-hearted lesbian relationship when I married him. I still accepted the current belief that homosexuality was deviant although, in my blood and bones, I felt quite different — that is, did not feel deviant. My relationship with my husband was quick and, for him, his first serious commitment. I believe I married him because there was so much enigma in his make-up — latent homosexuality which I did not then recognize! I have stayed married to him first because of the children, and secondly be-

cause he is *very* dependent on me. Thirdly, I am almost completely dependent on him financially.

She went on to write:

> [the children] might have been much better off if I had taken them and tried to get along as a single woman. But I had had two quite satisfactory (lesbian) relationships while I was bringing them up. Of course, for me, there was the usual dislike of living a lie and having to keep my devotion to my lover a secret. And there was the tension of not sharing a bed or the little household things we both loved to do for the other. But those kinds of tensions—or others like them—may be the spice that holds two women together in a monogamous tie.

Her husband "is curiously silent about homosexuality," and she presumes that because of his religious training "he looks on it as a sin. I suspect that he is a latent homosexual." She concluded:

> All this makes my life a juggling act. Most people I know don't know I'm a lesbian, but they know that I don't get along well with my husband. I often *long* to tell my closest friends and have recently told three of them. I still don't want my husband hurt.

COMING OUT

In current gay usage, "coming out" has several meanings. I found the term confusing when I first joined the lesbian community in San Francisco in the late 1970s.[10] It can mean: (a) a woman's first physical (not necessarily genital) experience with another woman; (b) her first realization of her own physical/emotional attraction to women; and (c) her announcement or admission of her lesbianism either to a limited circle of friends or to the public at large. One of our 60-plus generation described the process in her case:

I was attracted to several women in my twenties/thirties but never acted on it. In fact, I felt ashamed and embarrassed. When I was in therapy at age 47 or 48, I was finally able to acknowledge that it was a healthy, normal feeling. At 50, when I had my first sexual relationship with a woman, I was still relating to men. I became involved in feminist conscious-ness raising groups and worked as a member of a feminist counseling collective and gradually came to a decision to "come out" — *politically* — as I called it, because I wasn't in a relationship with a woman at the time.

Another "late-bloomer," in a heterosexual marriage for 31 years, stated:

My years (approximately 20) as a closeted woman-identified woman have been my strongest and most satisfying. When my acceptance as an open lesbian led to political and emotional growth, my sexuality was affected as well. Now, at 65, I feel flexibility, change, and acceptance of age and the inevitability of my own death far less terrifying than my nuclear-heterosex-ual and upper middle class, Jewish background formerly dic-tated.

A third respondent, having been in three conventional marriages, explained her quandary about "coming out":

I feel very "iffy" about my answers because I hardly see my-self as a lesbian yet. I had a strongly lesbian youth, then a strongly heterosexual stage, then survived on friendships for years, and am now just beginning to return to the passions of my youth. I recognized my lesbian cravings only [recently].

In answer to Question No. 34, "Since age 60, have your relation-ships with women differed from those you had before?" she noted: "I have been celibate since about 1970. Now (age 60) I am trying to 'come out' after the long dry spell and, before that, heterosexuality for 20-plus years."

A PERSONAL NOTE

"Coming out," in the sense of "going public," was something I did not do myself until 1977 when I rode in San Francisco's Lesbian and Gay Freedom Day Parade. I did so quite by accident, because I went only as an onlooker, being a newcomer to the city. A friend had invited me to join her in viewing the parade. However, an older lesbian I had recently met drove by, sitting on the back of a convertible under the Gray Panther's banner. She saw me on the curb and motioned for me to join her, which I did. My friend rode in the front seat beside the driver, while I sat ensconced beside the older woman.

Riding in the parade was an exhilarating experience, but not quite a complete "coming out." As noted above, I had used pseudonyms for excerpts from my memoirs published 2 years later. After 45 years as a university professor and civil servant, it was difficult for me to use my own name in print that reaches a much wider audience. At least in the parade I was anonymous. Now I am entirely "out of the closet," but, even so, with mixed feelings. Like so many lesbians of my generation, I am not comfortable with such a label. It does not describe my identity, which is still best delineated by the term "academic." However, now that my career cannot be affected, which was always my paramount concern, I am more "out" as a lesbian in order to help destroy the public stereotype of "dyke" as a mindless deviant, as well as to lessen the homophobia which accompanies it.

NOTES

1. Books on the subject of homosexuality, which had been medicalized by the first decade of the new century, were under lock and key in the pubic libraries and generally unavailable to the lay reader. For the book mentioned here, see Hall, R. (1982). *The well of loneliness*. London: Jonathan Cape, Ltd. (original work published 1928).

2. Only one of those who filled out our questionnaire checked the "yes" on our ex-nun query. See the book *Lesbian nuns: Breaking silence* for more recent revelations. Rosemary Curb & Nancy Manahan (Eds.) Tallahassee, FL: Naiad Press, 1985.

3. In spite of all the discouragement and restrictions, plus the added hin-

drance of age, the majority (58%) of our 60-plus respondents reported doing vigorous daily exercise.

4. In the earlier 65-plus survey, in answer to the question: "Were you considered a tomboy when you were a child?"(a question not included in the later 60-plus questionnaire), 37 out of the 50 polled answered "yes".

5. During their employment years, 91 of the 100 surveyed were "white collar" workers in the professional, clerical or business categories.

6. Boston Women's Health Collective. (1984). *The new our bodies, our selves*. New York: Simon & Shuster.

7. Adair, P., & Adair, N. (Producers & Directors). (1978). *The word is out* [film]. New York: Mariposa Film Group.

8. See my account of my own experience as a civil servant: Kehoe, M. (1985). An incident in the fifties, in M. Cruikshank (Ed.), *The lesbian path* (pp. 86-91, 182-186). San Francisco, CA: Grey Fox Press.

9. Butler, R.N., & Lewis, M.I. (1976). *Sex after sixty*. New York: Harper & Row, p. 112.

10. For a cogent political analysis of the subject, see Baetz, Ruth. (1984). The coming out process: Violence against lesbians, in T. Darty & S. Potter, (Eds.), *Women-identified women*. Palo Alto, CA: Mayfield.

Chapter 3

Family and Other Social Relationships

We have been learning in the 1980s that the family may be less than the ideal social institution that tradition and the pro-family activists have wanted us to believe. We hear more and more about incest, wife-beating, and child abuse in the home, topics not previously treated so openly by the media. One of the spin-offs of the feminist movement, and the establishment of shelters for battered women, has been to enable the victims of such abuse to speak up publicly about such molestations within the family circle.

Females have been the most frequent victims of child abuse. Some adult lesbians have had traumatic sexual experiences, at an early age, that have adversely affected their familial relationships as well as their attitude toward the opposite sex. Others, observing the brutalization of their mothers or sisters, developed a fear of marriage and became determined to avoid such abusive situations. Thus, as they grew up they found a less compelling need to suppress their affectional preference for those of their own more compassionate gender.

WITH PARENTS AND SIBLINGS

Quarreling between parents and divorce would undoubtedly raise questions in a thoughtful young girl's mind about the choice of marriage and homemaking as a career. A 70-year-old lesbian still asked herself, "I wonder what effect, *if any,* the divorce of my parents when I was 17, had on my lesbianism?" With the wider opportunity for women's economic independence in the first half of this century, those without means could begin to consider becoming self-supporting rather than entering the convent or the brothel. Fast food chains were not around to hire teenagers in large numbers, but there were typing and child-care jobs.

Family relationships sometimes became increasingly strained as the young women matured. Much of the stress existed and still exists between the lesbian and her siblings. Another septuagenarian had this comment:

> I regret that not once in my adult life could I ever establish rapport with my brother and my twin sister (the only relatives with whom I feel any ties) vis-à-vis my lesbianism, and our family relationship *was and is* one of total lack of communication on this entire subject. A blank wall stands between me and them and all three of us in growing old are unlikely to penetrate the wall. Now it is too late to matter.

As might be expected, brothers seem to have been especially threatened and intolerant of their deviant sisters. Half of the respondents who have nongay brothers report "seldom" or "never" having any contact with them, while those with married or nonsupportive sisters communicate with them somewhat more often.

WITH CHILDREN

The "late-blooming" lesbians who married and had families of their own (27 of the total) before realizing or admitting their gender preference were often later ostracized by their own adult nongay children. Some sons, as they matured, repudiated their mothers' life-style and more were out of contact with them than were the daughters. Many of the late bloomers made thoughtful observations on family life and expressed the joy their children had brought them. One who remained childless made a wry comment, "I do love kids — as long as they are not mine." On lesbians rearing children, another reflected:

> I found in my case that my son acquired some of his sex identification from his father, from me, and from my friend — [he] took on some of my friend's masculine characteristics — learned carpentry skills from me, for example — [and he]

turned out straight and monogamous. This made me suspect that children pick their identities from many close sources and the sex of the individual is not that important.

One respondent, with somewhat alienated heterosexual brothers and sisters, but with supportive sons and daughters who "relate to the same sex" themselves, raised the nature/nurture question, one which she finds puzzling because her parents (now deceased) had a 55-year marriage "in a good (emotionally and physically) relationship." She concluded, "I am sure, had I to do life over, that I would want children—that was an important part of my total development, as me—and that I would prefer, in the long run, being a lesbian."

A retired widow of a 28-year marriage admitted:

> I was never meant to lead the heterosexual life, but I rejected the idea of moving to New York and following a lesbian life in an environment that looked bleak in the forties. Opted instead to marry, although the marriage was not satisfactory for the obvious reason. But I was happy with my children and got pleasure out of living the establishment life. Until the end of the marriage, I had only one extremely brief same-sex involvement over that long, long period. It might well be different if the world had been what it is like now!

One rather exceptional story is that of the 70-year-old teacher, now retired and living alone, having been divorced after a 44-year marriage and eight children (plus 30 grandchildren and four great-grandchildren). All of her children have a "very negative" attitude toward their mother now that she is out of the closet, but she does receive some support from the one of her two brothers who is also gay.

WITH HUSBANDS

Relationships with husbands vary. One of the lesbians surveyed still maintains her marriage, but without deceit; her husband knows and chooses to ignore his wife's "affair." The rest of the late bloomers are separated, divorced, or widowed. One divorcee has not made up her mind to return completely to the "passions of my youth." Fourteen have had second conventional marriages and four have had three. (I say "conventional" because some lesbians of the younger generation do "marry" each other with rites comparable to those of the legally recognized male/female union.)

In at least one instance, a widowed homemaker had found her husband her best supporter and friend during their years together. She had a particularly accommodating household. Both of them, along with their young son and the mother's female partner, lived together congenially, with the father and son occupying one floor of their suburban home while the two women had the other. Of course, all socialized together in their free time. The son grew up under "aunty's" love and supervision, having two mothers as well as a caring male parent. Now, at middle age himself, the son continues to have a warm relationship with his mother, who is alone, and his father. Aunty died of cancer more than a decade ago. Admittedly, this kind of mutually accommodating relationship may have been extraordinary for the mid-20th century and was probably difficult to sustain over the years in a suburban neighborhood, but it is a testimonial to the adaptation possible in what may appear to be the "nuclear family."

WITH OTHER MEN AND WOMEN

Reflections on their experience with both kinds of relationships by our late bloomers reveal their preference and why. One said relationships with women are "much more caring, understanding, mutually supporting, non-competitive." Another pointed out that she "can relate emotionally to a woman on a more spiritual level." A third thinks that, "Women are more gentle, thoughtful, and unselfish than men." Still others commented:

> Communication is far easier with a woman. Women "speak my language," men don't.

> Women are more sensitive, intuitive, considerate . . . far less "set," rigid, or uncompromising. They are more generous

with time, attention and *caring*. They are more willing to share feelings, emotions, even worldly goods.

With a woman there is the more complete attitude of caring about the whole person.

With my husband, after a while, there was no affective relationship.

Life with a woman is probably more precarious and vulnerable than married life with a man, but much less threatening and more comfortable.

One woman expressed a slightly different view: "Women without men or the experience of relationships with them sometimes seem dry, frigid, and incomplete."

Without supportive family relationships, either as children growing up "different" or as older women "coming-out" after years of conventional married life, lesbians in their sixth decade and beyond seek social networks among those who share their preferred lifestyle. Sixty-one of our respondents associate almost exclusively with other lesbians, while 30 include heterosexual women among their closest friends. Only two relate to gay men, and none seem to include heterosexual men as close friends.

We do not know how many of the 100 women who participated in the 1984 survey may consider themselves separatists: the question was not asked. However, the earlier (1980-1983) research did include the specific question: "Are you a separatist?" Forty of the 50 surveyed said that they were *not*. (Eight checked "Don't know," and one wrote in the margin, "What's a separatist?") This seems in direct contradiction to the information on friendship patterns gathered in the later study, even though the same respondents were included. Such different results point out the need for interviewing in this kind of research in order to clarify ambiguities, misinterpretation of questions, or unfamiliarity with the terminology used. It is likely that many of these "post-adult" lesbians escaped the political thrust of the feminist movement of the 1970s that focused on men as the oppressors; thus, they were puzzled by the term "separatist."

SENIOR CENTERS

Outside the family, social life for lesbians over 60 seems to be more or less restricted not only to their own kind, but also to their own age group. Ninety-five report associating with those within 10 years of their own age, and 60 belong or have belonged to lesbian-only or lesbian/gay groups. Only seven say they have met other lesbians in bars, which the majority do not frequent. Most do not use the mainline senior centers or take part in their programs. In spite of the fact that half live in urban areas, where such centers are most likely to exist, only five use them regularly. Only one (me) indicates she eats there daily, but my own experience with senior centers is probably not the average. All the regular patrons of my "nutrition site" (as it is called by the Commission on Aging that funds it) know about my life-style because I appeared there on a GLOE (Gay and Lesbian Outreach to Elders) panel designed to acquaint seniors with our organization. Only one woman (who no longer attends) seemed unable to accept someone who she perceived as a "queer." She asked me not to sit at her table because she said she didn't like to eat with "freaks." All the rest of the clientele treat me just as they did before my appearance as a GLOE advocate. Even though I do not socialize with them except for superficial dinner conversation, they are all pleasant and congenial. We have few interests in common—theirs being mostly ailments, grandchildren, deceased spouses, church activities, and bingo. This kind of difference in background may be the reason, at least in part, why our respondents do not use mainline senior centers. It should be noted that many do not have such facilities in their area, so the question applied mainly to those in urban areas.

INFORMAL GATHERINGS

The 60-plus lesbian seems to rely, rather, on small informal social gatherings of her own kind. One expressed some disappointment, though, with this particular form of socializing. "I was in an informal group of this kind, mostly losers, and it took away some of my optimism." Some lesbians of the older generation object to the confessional-type meetings often conducted by the 35-plus crowd at their SOL (Slightly Older Lesbians) get-togethers. Such personal revelations make the older women uncomfortable. They are hesitant to air their feelings before a group of strangers made up of young women the same ages as their own children. A few others expressed disenchantment with their experience of these "special interest" meetings. One who came out when she was over 50 admitted:

> I have never felt part of a lesbian community. For several years I attended meetings and social events, but I never felt at home there. I finally decided that I came to this too late in life — too set in a lifetime of other ways. There is an ingrown closed quality in lesbian groups and in their relationships that bothers me. I understand its roots, but it makes me uneasy.

Another late bloomer had a different objection. She said that since she reached 60, she has discovered it is

> more difficult to find lesbian-oriented women who are really fun to be with over a period of time. They seem to be so many "old maids" (stiff-minded), permanently planted, unimaginative, unadventurous, and lacking a desire to grow spiritually. Many have given up their quest. I now have more straight women friends and companions for these reasons.

In view of the fact that the active lesbian community is small, even in the coastal municipalities where the largest number of gay people reside, it is understandable that not all find each other compatible. Nevertheless, their gatherings at each other's homes provide an outlet for a very closeted group of older women, most of whom are retired and thus cut off from the social contacts they formerly had in the work place. And what do these aging women do for recreation when they get together? Those in couples mention attending concerts, visiting museums or art galleries, and going to the theater. Others enjoy outdoor activities such as camping or picnicking. Long walks and hiking attract some of the more athletic. At parties held in each others' homes, they dance, play pool, cards, trivial pursuits, or other table games. (Personally, I like to invite friends over for ping-pong parties.)

LESBIAN AND GAY ORGANIZATIONS
FOR SENIORS

The established organizations for older lesbians, where they exist, have dances for members and their friends, along with potluck dinners and outings to nearby places of interest. They arrange rap sessions, support groups, writers' and actors' workshops, and other social programs. Most of these activities, which are promoted largely by public-funded organizations and serve gays of both sexes, are usually more successful when their activities are segregated. Even though they may not perceive themselves as separatists, lesbians and gay men over 60 seem to prefer participating in social activities separately. This is not surprising in view of their choice of life-style, but organizers sometimes feel that more effort should be made to unite the two factions for mutual support. This is true, of course, politically. But it doesn't work socially.

LONELINESS AND ISOLATION

In spite of all these opportunities for socializing, there are always those who have lost a partner, live alone, or are isolated, and have more leisure time than they can fill. On rainy days or for long evenings, they read, watch TV, or listen to music. Many have hobbies (gardening is a favorite), while others paint or write. More than half (57) of the respondents live alone. Many are out of reach of any special social/recreational facilities designed for them. It is no wonder, then, that loneliness is the "most serious problem" for those who answered the questionnaire.

Although loneliness and isolation are prime causes of deep distress and, frequently, of suicide among the elderly, we can only speculate how many, if any, of the more than one million American women over 60 who identify as lesbians do commit suicide. Lifestyle is not indicated on death certificates, and families, who "take over" at these times, are reluctant to admit or recognize the relationship the deceased may have had with her "roommate."

Those who participated in our study are survivors, coping with loneliness and the aging process rather well. But they are, as we have already noted, a select group. Many of the most vulnerable did not hear of the study, so could not be involved. Some of those who did fill out the questionnaire had poignant comments scribbled in the margin. In answer to "What is your present living arrangement?" a 70-year-old from a rural area in the Middle West wrote, "I live with my black-and-white cat," and added that she travels more than 100 miles monthly to attend SOL meetings in the nearest city, just to have some contact with people she can relate to. Another of the same age from the South, who checked loneliness as her worst problem, noted that her need is "not for more friends, but for someone of my own." She went on to tell us, "My roommate died in 1981 and I have been alone since," and she concluded, "I wonder if finding someone isn't the biggest problem for older lesbians who are not in large cities." One woman, 68 when she answered our questionnaire and whose "partner" had died 8 years earlier, described the loss with intense feeling, then wrote:

> My heart and mind are still with it all, but here I am in this damnable aging process and lonely, taking painting instruction to get out and see people — all of them heterosexual with husbands, wives, kids, doing all the folksy things I've never related to, having never been a pot holder.

In answer to our request for comments on the questionnaire, another simply asked, "Where can I meet other older lesbians?"[1]

Isolation can cause distress even when women are in an otherwise satisfactory couple relationship. One told us that her partner is in poor health and lives 30 miles away in a rural area. Both have aged cars and there is no public transportation, so they must remain alone much of the time. Another small town resident, unfamiliar with "The Wishing Well,"[2] remarked: "We need a gay correspondence club to break this wall of loneliness. There are about 20,000 gays (men and women) in my state. All I need is one."

The question, "How would you describe your emotional health?" brought, for example, this reply: "Excellent, except I want a partner." Another we asked, "Who would help you or take care of you if you were very ill or disabled?" was answered "Don't know" by one who wrote in the margin, "This worries me a good deal." Although she is employed part-time and seems to be coping, that respondent lamented:

> All my friends have someone else who is No. 1 in their lives. I'm lucky to be No. 3, 4, or 10, and my self-esteem suffers accordingly, not to mention my social life. I'd be in real trouble if it weren't for the Temple.

She derives support from her religion, as do a few others, from organizations like Dignity, for example. However, most have abandoned the comfort of the patriarchal churches that still view homosexuality as a sin. Some continue in satisfactory social relationships with former lovers and find relief from loneliness in friendship. An 80-year old told us, "I presently have no relationship other than friends. Up until I was 65, I had a close relationship with a former lover. We are friends now, good friends—no physical contact other than an occasional welcoming or goodbye kiss."

In answer to the question, "Have you ever felt discriminated against within the lesbian community because of your age?" a lifelong lesbian pushing 90 reassured us, "I have more friends now than when I was younger." Another replied to the same question even more succinctly: "What community?" A retired teacher has had a different experience, which she expressed rather ruefully:

> I can be friends with gay men because I won't get hurt emotionally, and, some are caring and helpful, but with lesbians I'm like a kid in a candy store with no money. They just want me out of the way.

One member of a couple who had been together for 32 years pointed out that many friends have dropped out of her life since her retirement. She and her partner, who is 5 years older, are seeking out new "old" friends, but she wrote that "It is increasingly difficult to find friends our age who are not always bitching about their health or fighting World War II all over again."

AGE MATES

Although a few lesbians who have passed their 60th birthdays enjoy intergenerational relationships and friends, the majority, as we have mentioned, prefer to socialize with people their own age. The stereotype of the old lesbian corrupting young girls is certainly not supported by the findings of this study. One respondent was quite specific: "My lesbian friends here are all under 40—unfortunately. I would be just as interested as you (referring to our survey) in locating older ones." In another margin note, she wrote:

> The majority of my local friends are much younger than I. Most are lesbian, but a few are not. Other friends, neighbors, and even family have expressed great surprise at this since they don't know of the lesbian angle, but most think it is fine. I would like to see my young friends more often, but they are very busy working, studying, spending weekends with their families or otherwise out of town, engaging in sports I can't really share (running, softball, volleyball, etc.). Most of them are coupled, so [they] always have each other and don't need me as much as I need them.

A lifelong lesbian, now over 70, had an upbeat comment, "I have never known many lesbians until 4 years ago when I made my new lesbian friends. It was liberating!"

RETIREMENT

Gerontology deals with many aspects of aging, including retirement. Sixty of the 100 lesbians in our survey are retired. For many elderly people (especially males) retirement can be traumatic—an identity crisis, as many describe it. It is sometimes the same for older lesbians who have been in professional jobs that gave them status and where they relied more on their work associates for social interaction. In contrast, women who have been homemakers usually relate to their relatives more intensively in later years.

Professional workers are among those with the highest degree of job satisfaction. Therefore, they might be expected to suffer the most severe loss upon retirement, when they leave the position that gave them stature. However, our well-educated, reasonably healthy, and financially comfortable professional lesbians seem to have adjusted to their changed status more easily. One exception, formerly in the legal profession, said she "feels more discrimination because of being retired rather than aging. People tend to turn off when they hear I'm retired." Few of the others who are retired commented on it either favorably or unfavorably; thus, we can only assume that the majority have adapted without too much pain. One who was a university professor and now lives in a retirement center with 300 other residents, indicated her most serious problem is "not daring to decloset." She said nothing about any other disadvantages of her retirement.

COMMUNITY LIVING

Apropos our inquiry into the subject of community living[3] in old age, the majority preferred a retirement center ("if necessary") designed for lesbians only. Indeed, several efforts have been made in different parts of the country to establish such communities specifically for elderly or frail lesbians. It seems to have been a movement begun only recently as the aged population grows and gains more awareness in our society. Two informants who are in need of such a facility pled, "Please find me one!" On the other hand, the attitude toward nursing homes is more negative. One expressed an extreme antipathy: "The thought of being in a nursing home terrifies me. My mother is in a board-and-care which is bad enough. I've been a volunteer in a nursing home. It's *hell*." Even a retirement community does not meet with universal approval. A 70-plus respondent, still living in her own home, had this observation: "By a retirement community I assume you mean it would be for older people only. I do not wish this." Another described her reaction more volubly: "I just turned 65 and have received more 'senior city' (hate that word) crap that all goes in file No. 9 (wastebasket) unopened." It is understandable that most of us who are healthy may not be ready to contemplate the time when we will lose some of our independence and find it necessary to rely on others for help in making decisions about our lives. But there are obviously others who would welcome community living in which they could participate with their own kind in mutual support.

The social life of those lesbians over 60 who are in couples (43 of those surveyed) tends to be even less public than that of those who are single. The couples stay together and tend to rely on each other as they age. They apparently have less need to socialize, and are not "cruising" — as the younger gay men and women describe those seeking a partner. In a more stable relationship, they often seem to prefer staying at home to enjoy quiet times together. They are the ones who are more likely to flee the city after retirement, especially those who have spent many years together, and buy a house in the suburbs or in the country where they can grow artichokes or zinnias, keep bees, or just rusticate. They are the truly hidden ones.[4]

LIFE SATISFACTION

Social life for lesbians born in the early 1920s or before varies as it does for all their female contemporaries. Some, afflicted with illness or physical handicaps, will lead more restricted lives. Others, with very limited incomes and few resources, will also suffer social limitations. The women surveyed and reported on here are not among those who have experienced severe hardships. They have apparently learned to cope with nonsupportive families in a generally homophobic environment. Although often lonely, they have been able to hook into sympathetic networks or find partners for survival in a hostile world. They are the lucky ones who may serve as models for a new generation of women who have chosen an alternate life-style. The overall adjustment of the majority of this group is reflected in their scores on the Life Satisfaction Inventory that was included in the questionnaire. Thirty-eight made the top percentile (11-13), and 48 were in the middle group (6-10), while the remaining 14 viewed life less agreeably as they aged.

Since 1961, social gerontologists have been talking about the theory of disengagement that holds, among other things, that the process of withdrawing from society is typical of aging persons. However, most of the lesbians involved here have, as we have seen, sustained a relatively high morale and level of life satisfaction in the face of many difficulties and rejections. They (especially those not in couples) would therefore seem to support the activity theory, which holds the contrary position; namely, that maintaining substantial levels of physical, mental, and social activity is generally part of successful aging. Thirty-two percent are still employed either full- or part-time. At least some of the strength of the lesbians surveyed lies in the fact that they represent an advantaged group: well-educated, in good health, and economically self-sufficient. Even when they are lonely or isolated, they still seek companionship and desire to relate to others. They are not loners by choice. Just how healthy, wealthy and wise they have managed to be in their later years we shall see in the following chapters.

NOTES

1. For a nationwide list of organizations and services for older lesbians and gay men, one can write to A. J. Lucco, MD, Levindale Geriatric Center, 2434 W. Belvedere Avenue, Baltimore, MD 21215-5299.

2. A nationwide lesbian correspondence service based in Napa, CA.

3. For a recent survey report on "Planned Retirement Housing Preferences of Older Gay Men and Lesbians," contact A. J. Lucco, MD, Levindale Geriatric Center, 2434 W. Belvedere Avenue, Baltimore, MD 21215-5299.

4. For an answer to the question, "Which factors in the aging process are different for homosexuals because of their life-style choices?", see Lipman, A. (1986, Summer). Homosexual Relationships. *Generations*, pp. 51-55.

Chapter 4

Lesbian Relationships and Homosexuality

In 1977, Dr. Elliot Feigenbaum, a San Francisco psychiatrist, wrote in his article, "Sexual Behavior in the Later Years,"[1] that "some people are still aghast at the thought of sexual relationships" between the elderly. He was, of course, referring to heterosexual relations. He further pointed out that greater permissiveness "in recent years" has come "to include such behavior." Even now, he wrote, "the issue is still one that can upset professionals and laymen alike." But he concluded that "many people who can accept heterosexual relationships" between those in this advanced age group find that "homosexual relationships or sexual relationships between old and young are very distressing" (p. 91). The incredible idea of homosexual relationships between the young *and* old is not even suggested, yet 29 of our 100 subjects have had relationships with women more than 10 years younger (some as much as half their age), although the majority did express a preference for those within 10 years of their own age. The following comment from one respondent reflected a common complaint: "Finding a partner—I cannot accept someone more than 15 years younger and don't seem to meet any older, unattached women."

The gravity of the taboo on physical relationships of this kind is still hardly imaginable. The insistence that sexual activity should be engaged in for procreative rather than recreative purposes continues to prevail. Negative cultural stereotypes of sexual behavior for women in old age also persist—even when such considerations no longer matter. Conventional thinking holds that sexual activity either does not exist after the onset of "old age" (seldom specifically defined), or that it shouldn't. As one respondent stated, "We are regarded as doddering old souls to be humored, and we are not supposed to have a sex life or even think of it!'' Studies of the sexuality of older women are few, and those of lesbians over 60 years old almost nil. We are exploring a new area of inquiry dealing with a population that grew up in a ''neurotically conditioned culture'' regarding sex.

For those who participated in our 1984 survey, 74 described their sexual history as either (a) exclusively homosexual (39), or (b) mainly homosexual but with incidental heterosexual experience (12). Seventy-seven said they had had emotional relationships only with women, while 62 had engaged in physical/sexual activity with women only. About the same number (63) had erotic fantasies involving women exclusively. Sixty-six indicated that they were currently sexually active. Of those currently celibate, two thirds admitted it was not by choice. Because the majority reported good or excellent health, it is perhaps surprising that more than half had had no sexual activity with another woman in the past year. Yet when we recall that 57 live alone, 10 with a ''friend,'' 4 with relatives, and 5 with ''other,'' it becomes evident that this self-restraint may instead be a result of lack of opportunity, isolation, or inconvenience.

BEFORE AND AFTER 60

Lest these statistics seem to buttress the widely held notion that all homosexuals are obsessed with the physical aspects of their relationships, it should be noted that most lesbians, as they mature, regard the emotional aspects as more important. In response to the question (No. 43), ''Before age 60, how important was sex to you in a lesbian relationship?'' only one checked that it was the main part. Eighty-four rated sex as one important part, while 13 considered it unimportant and two said that no sex was involved.

In contrast to the *before*-60 assessment, the *after*-60 result was as follows: 72 rated sex as one important part; 28 said it is unimportant. None considered it the main or significant part of her relationship. The second part of Question No. 34, which asked how their relationships differed after they reached 60, brought some illuminating comments. For some, relationships are quieter, more stable, less intense, sometimes less physical. Few fall in love anymore. Friendship and intimacy are more important and satisfying than sex to most. Some reported that they are less sexual out of inhibition or caution, while others said they find sex boring. One woman wrote, "My partner, who had always been the aggressor, gradually lost her libido, due to menopause and probably the onset of cancer, so our sexual relationship ceased. My present relationship with lesbians, all young, is emotional but not sexual." Others wrote:

No physical contact.

More friendship, less sex.

Short affairs, no deep feeling.

Bonding seems more difficult to maintain.

The earlier affairs were with women who subsequently married men. The recent one was with a declared lesbian.

Love but no sex.

As a younger woman I was strongly attracted to women older than myself. After age 60 I am attracted to women younger than myself.

Deeper feeling—even more sexually satisfying.

Less sexual love-making, more communication, more romance.

I always play straight.

More cautious and reluctant to be sexually involved until I am sure I love the person.

I no longer look for sexual relationships. I maintain very good friendly relationships with two former lovers.

One dissident commented that her relationship is "deeper and more emotional, also much more sexual."

We see from these remarks the wide variety of attitudes expressed as the relationship changed after age 60. Because the majority of the respondents left the second part of Question No. 34 blank (which asked for an explanation of the difference), while a few skipped the question altogether, the answers summarized above are from those who completed the question and specified the difference between their relationships *before* and *after* they reached 60 years of age. The relatively small number who filled in both parts of the question may have resulted from the reluctance of the others to amplify the details of such a personal part of their lives. It is notable, too, that no comments were appended to the section on sexuality, which two skipped altogether. In general, then, because only one found her relationship "more sexually satisfying" *after* 60, and only one other claimed "a much more sexual" relationship then, we may conclude that sex is not necessarily the principal preoccupation of this age group of lesbians. A late bloomer put it this way:

> At this point in my life I don't think of myself as a lesbian. I am a person who loves/feels affectionate in a nonsexual way. The fire hasn't totally gone out, but it's unlikely now that sex can be a very large — or even any — part of my life.

LESBIAN IDENTITY AND SEX

Now may be a good point at which to say something about the use of the term "lesbian" to describe the participants in the study reported on here. The common usage of the word to designate a woman whose affectional/sexual preference is for another woman is so widespread that it almost seems redundant to restrict the term to its more appropriate adjectival position — as in "lesbian woman." Nevertheless, the homosexual behavior associated with the word does not necessarily constitute an identity. For most female homosexuals, being a lesbian is only an extracurricular part of their lives, just as being nongay is with heterosexuals who are not, as a rule, designated solely by their preference for a sleeping partner. More often, people are identified by their occupations, what they do for a living — musicians, lawyers, teachers, farmers, homemakers, and so on.

In answer to Question No. 2, "What word do you *prefer* to use to describe your emotional and/or sexual preference?" a retired P.E. teacher wrote, "Anything but 'lesbian.' The word conjures up jeans, boots, men's shirts, rough, loud-talking, intimidating females trying to look and act like men but doing a damned poor job of it." One "unattached" late bloomer, somewhat less emphatic, stated:

> I think I would not like to be identified by sexual preference — either as a homosexual or a heterosexual. Gay refers more to a subculture. I don't separate love and sex, but homosexuality is more likely to be a love deviation than a sexual one since most people can achieve orgasm in a variety of ways.

The AIDS epidemic has made "homosexual" a term of even more severe opprobrium for males, a stigma, which in the public mind, is often extended to females, although the concern has always been, especially in the case of the generation dealt with here, focused more on the emotional/affectional aspects of relationships rather than on the physical/genital. Seventy-eight of the 100 women surveyed expressed a positive attitude toward monogamy. The promiscuity of their male counterparts has been a source of wonder and even embarrassment to many lesbians of the older generation. A former nurse, now retired, expressed it simply by writing, "I have difficulty accepting male homosexuality and the idea of sodomy." For many who grew up in an era that didn't speak of such things, the "idea of sodomy" generally meant anal intercourse, which they found as repugnant as did some of their heterosexual peers.

BISEXUALITY

Although, as we have seen, many late bloomers have married or had sexual relations with men, only nine of the 100 surveyed identified themselves as bisexuals. A psychiatric social worker, still fully employed at the time of filling out the questionnaire, explained that "[I] have always thought of myself as bisexual. Did not marry (heterosexual) until age 42. Have always been monogamous, whether in lesbian or heterosexual relationships. At age 50 I chose to spend the rest of my life as a lesbian.

According to their history, some have considered themselves bisexual because they were formerly married, even though they have been in a monogamous lesbian relationship for many years. A sexually active 66-year old, never-married, who classified herself as "bisexual," commented on her earlier life by writing, "Perhaps had I been with a man/married, I would prefer that, but I think I am still more emotionally comfortable in relationships with women." She went on to conclude, "If a man could arouse me as a woman does, I might enjoy him as much sexually." Another 75-plus respondent, never married, who identifies as a bisexual, is in a 30-year-plus lesbian relationship in which she has been celibate for the last 10 years. She described it as "a deep love relationship, very private — one is *alive* and blessed with a partner of 30 years." A 75-year-old widow of a 37-year conventional marriage calls herself "bisexual" evidently because of a 2-year relationship with an older woman half a century earlier. Such varied interpretations of the term "bisexual" emphasizes again the importance of interviewing for eliciting reliable data from informants. In all the cases reviewed in this survey, none of the individuals who checked the term "bisexual" as the word they preferred to describe their emotional and/or sexual preference were relating to both sexes at the same time.[2]

COUPLES

Forty-three of our respondents answered "yes" to the question: "Are you *currently* involved in a relationship with a woman?" Of these, the three longest had lasted 56, 55, and 40 years each; eight had been maintained for over 30 years, two for 35. Six had been in their present relationship for less than one year, but most of these had had an ongoing partner, in some cases now deceased, for longer periods in the past. A few were exulting in new relationships. The mean length of all was 13.5 years. Nine are the younger member of a couple.

Of the remaining majority (56) who are or were uncoupled (in 1984), one had previously been in a relationship for 44 1/2 years, one for 32 years, and five for 20 years or longer. In their case, the mean duration was 15 years. The age difference between the members of all the couples ranged from 0 (in only one case were both the same age) to 40 years (in two cases). Seventy-seven were the older member, and 18 the younger. Four either did not answer the question or had been both younger and older in different dyads. Those who had lost a partner by death (20) had many disturbing experiences and concerns — emotional, legal, social, and economic. One who had lost an older lover of 15 years explained her anguish:

> I became a hermit. For at least a year I wept when I looked at anyone — this I hid — but I still become depressed. For several years I frequently visited the mausoleum and talked to her (No one else around). My work is my savior.

Another, also the younger member of a couple who had been together 40 years, had a comforting experience during her grieving. "The loss was so emotional that, for the first time, I told my friends of our relationship — and all accepted it with sympathy." The survivor of the couple that had lived together for 44 1/2 years admits that her most serious problem is still loneliness, long after the woman she loved died. "I miss my companion. She made it like Christmas every day. She made my life worthwhile."

An example of the legal problems and difficulties that can occur with the family of the deceased is explained by a woman who had been named the beneficiary of her lover's part in the house and business they had owned together:

> Her will is being contested by her family and the property we had in joint ownership is in litigation. Even the burial plans were overruled by them, and they finally made the medical decision to remove her life support systems.

The devastation of losing the most important person in one's life can also have its physical effects. On the aftermath of such an experience, another respondent said, "I've since retired and through all the stress of this negativism have a chronic lung problem." Another retiree, who lost a "spouse" 6 years her junior, reported, "Death was sudden and unexpected and, after 14 years, a terrific blow. I suffered all the usual emotions of the bereaved spouse — felt deserted, angry, lonely, anxious."

Of course, the lesbian relationships of some of our respondents were terminated for other reasons besides death, and often just as painfully.[3]

Although no research specifically designed to assess the factors that enhance the same-sex relationships of women over 60 has been done, answers to various questions in this survey offer hints as to the satisfaction those studied have derived from their liaisons. First of all, 71 feel very positive about their lesbianism, and 82 report they are in good or excellent emotional health. In spite of unhappy female/male marriages, loss of lovers by death, unwanted celibacy, aging, and debilitating illness, the majority fall above the mean score on the Life Satisfaction Scale. One 75-year-old former teacher, currently in a relationship, voiced her gratification:

> I'm exceedingly happy with my present relationship. My lover is considerate, mature, very loving. We have settled into a most comfortable retirement together – 17 wonderful years. We both pray we'll meet our Creator at the same time and have it over quick. We are blessed with good health, and I think we have 15-20 good years left yet.

One of the returned questionnaires was filled out for the couple: "Count this for two – both the same" is inscribed across the top. Born in 1904 and 1905, respectively, they met when they were 23 and 24 and have lived together ever since:

> Although we were rooming together during our senior year of college, there had not been any sex between us until near the end of that year. I remember thinking then, "I don't care. I have what I really want" – a great deal of love, deep concern for each other, tenderness, kisses, holding each other and talking together, making love by looking at each other's eyes with the love light in them.

In general, the coupled women in this survey (again, admittedly not a representative sample) have had the intelligence and good fortune to achieve happiness from their long-term relationships. Without a model, other than the traditional heterosexual marriage, many of them have been able to establish a balance of power and a division of activities for a model of their own, one closely resembling that of "best friends." They have preferred a steady, durable, monogamous love bond rather than casual encounters. They want companionship and affection, together with enduring tenderness and concern.

Obviously, sex is not the sole basis for their attachments. For the majority, commitment and compatibility are far more important. Out of the 100 surveyed, 53 had had no sexual experience with another woman in the past year. Some of this celibacy was, as has been pointed out before, not by choice, but for lack of opportunity. Nevertheless, with the exception of one or two cases, the emphasis in the back-page comments, where respondents were asked to append "anything else you would like to tell us about your life experience as a lesbian," was never on sexuality. It is evidently not their major concern. Growing up before the sexual revolution of the 1960s, they appear to have practiced sexual exclusivity even in their earlier relationships. If they changed partners several times in their youth, their sexual history remains one of serial monogamy without the sexual openness of the later era or of many homosexual men of their generation.[4]

Shere Hite, in her nationwide study of female sexuality,[5] included a chapter on "Lesbianism" in which she averred that:

> Homosexuality, or the desire to be physically intimate with someone of one's own sex at some time, or always, during one's life, can be considered a natural and "normal" variety of life experience. It is "abnormal" only when you posit as normal and healthy only an interest in reproductive sex. Discussion of why one becomes *heterosexual* would come to the same nonconclusions. (p. 392)

Hite went on to explain that "the prohibition on the exchange of physical contact (of any kind) between women is bound to increase the hostility and distance between them" (p. 392). To counteract the alienation, she concluded, "it is important for women to recognize their own potential for having sexual feelings for other women. If we want to grow strong, we must learn to love, respect, honor, and be attentive to and interested in other women" (p. 416).

If such a point of view had been as openly and widely expressed a half century ago, many gay women of our generation who had difficulties accommodating their own emotional needs would have found more support. Instead, we all had the medical treatment approach to what was then considered an illness, the last of the three historical conceptions of homosexuality — a sin, a crime, a sickness. The notion that homosexuality is a psychological deviance that must be cured was the prevalent view through the first half of the 20th century. During that period, many homosexuals, both women and men, internalized the conventional attitudes and became guilt-ridden patients of the perpetrators of their oppression.

Now, as the century comes to a close, we can hope that the same-sex intimacy characterized by the term "lovers" can have an increasing legitimacy as society becomes less homophobic and moves toward a new broader and more humane definition of human relations.

NOTES

1. Feigenbaum, E., in R.A. Kalish (Ed.), *The later years: Social applications of gerontology* (pp. 91-97). Belmont, CA: Wadsworth.

2. Berger used the term "ambisexual" to refer to those gay men who are both married to a woman and involved in homosexual relationships. See p. 197 of *Gay and gray*.

3. For the dissolution of lesbian relationships among younger lesbians, see the chapter on "Gay Divorce" in Mendola, M. (1980). *The Mendola report: A new look at gay couples* (Chap. 7, pp. 136-159). New York: Crown.

4. For research on the practices of younger lesbians today, see the "Symposium on Couples" issue of the *Journal of Homosexuality*, 8(2) (Winter 1982).

5. Hite, S. (1976). *The Hite Report*. New York: Dell.

Chapter 5

The Present:
Growing Old
(1950-1980)

The Korean War decade of the 1950s saw the rise of McCarthyism and the investigations of the House of Representatives Un-
American Activities Committee. Homosexuals were purged from
the State Department as security risks. A fever of antideviance
swept the country. In 1953, the same year that Kinsey and his associates published the relevations of diversity in *Sexual Behavior in
the Human Female*,[1] President Eisenhower signed Executive Order
No. 010450, the aim of which was to keep all "perverts" off the
government payroll.

Against this background of antagonism and oppression, the first
lesbian liberation organization in the United States, the Daughters
of Bilitis (DOB), was begun in 1955 by Del Martin and Phyllis
Lyon of San Francisco. Three years later, Barbara Gittings founded
a New York chapter of the organization and later became one of the
editors of its periodical publication, *The Ladder*, which was printed
from 1956 to 1972 and became a rallying ground and network of
lesbian support across the nation.

The 1960s saw the social pendulum swing toward liberalism. The
sexual revolution, the development of a counterculture, the Civil
Rights Bill of 1964, and the Vietnam antiwar protests all contributed to wider social change, from which the homophile movement
learned and benefited. The founding of the Metropolitan Community Church in southern California in 1968, together with the rise of
The Advocate as a significant gay publication, were further important steps on the way to the formation of the resistance that ex-

ploded in the Stonewall riot in New York City in 1969, the event which marked the birth of Gay Pride.

The Feminist Movement of the 1970s, and particularly the 1971 decision of the National Organization for Women (NOW) to support homosexual rights, had an equally important impact on the development of lesbian and gay politics. The National Gay Task Force (NGTF) was established in 1973, and by 1974 the American Psychiatric Association conceded that homosexuality was no longer to be diagnosed as a sickness — rather, only as a personality disorder.

To infer that all midlife or older lesbians of these decades were affected by, or even aware of, all the events that were gradually taking place to liberalize public attitudes would be a gross exaggeration. As Chapter 2 suggests, most lesbians were (and many still are) in the closet, largely insulated, except in metropolitan areas, from many of the events and circumstances that were affecting their younger, more actively involved sisters on both the West and East coasts. Homophobia continued unabated in rural and mid-America. In this study, we heard from the survivors, those who are by now mostly out of the closet, reasonably healthy, and emotionally stable.

But then, aging females — much less aging lesbians — were still of little concern to anybody else. For example, the *Hite Report* on female sexuality, which created such a stir in 1976, included fewer than 20 subjects (out of 1,066) who acknowledged being 60 years of age or older, and the very enlightened chapter on "Lesbianism" ignored the age factor altogether, while the chapter on "Older Women" did the same for their sexual preference. Most of Hite's older women supported the current view that sex can be enjoyed as long as one lives and remains in good health. However, the physical and mental health problems that often accompany old age can interfere.

PHYSICAL HEALTH

Fortunately, the majority of the 60-plus lesbians who took part in our study rated themselves in reasonably "good" (35) or "excellent" (37) physical health. Nevertheless, almost half (46) consider themselves "too fat" (three wrote in "obese"), while four said they were "too thin," the latter as a result of cancer or alcoholism.

Nine have recovered from major surgery (including one breast implant), and seven reported the same for disabling injuries. Arthritis (17) and hypertension (13) were the most frequently mentioned ailments, with coronary (6), thyroid problems (5), and allergies (4), following in that order. Three suffer from emphysema and the same number from diabetes. Impaired vision, with glaucoma as the culprit, also affects three. Osteoporosis, stroke, and Parkinson's disease claim one each.

Even with all these infirmities, the majority (53) said they have none that seriously restrict their activities. More than half (61) take medications, including aspirin and other mild analgesics. Their vision (with glasses) is "excellent" (44), "good" (41), or "fair" (13), while only one suffers "poor" vision. More than half (53) also reported "excellent" hearing (without an aid). Of the remainder, 29 claimed "good," 13 "fair" audition, and five hear "poorly" (without an aid). Mobility (without assistance) is even less of a problem. Seventy-six have no impediment to their walking. Sixteen get about with little detriment, and four have a slight handicap, while three are restricted. Alcoholism affects only 10, while 25 do not drink any alcoholic beverage (including beer and wine). The other 65 are social drinkers who have wine with meals or imbibe an occasional cocktail before dinner. Sixty-six, a large number for their generation, do not smoke at all. None smoke pot. Fifty-eight assured us that they exercise daily, while another 20 asserted that they are strenuously active at least once a week.

For the 75-year-old woman who is healthy and wants to continue her sports activities, the physical deterioration of aging is more difficult to adjust to than it is for the person who has not regularly participated in such strenuous exercise. Because many old lesbians have been "jocks" in their youth and expressed their "tomboy" personalities in competitive sports, the onset of old age — when the tennis court seems to have expanded to twice its original size, the mile jog seems more like five, the volleyball weighs as much as a medicine ball — is a painful experience in more than just the physical sense. They feel the loss of muscle power and prompt reaction response more keenly than their less active peers, and they may attempt to do more than their physical equipment can handle. They recall how many times their friends have told them, "It's time you slowed down.'' Maybe Kathryn Hepburn's solution (in her late 70s) for her tennis game is a good idea. She allows herself two bounces, while her younger opponent must play the larger doubles court on one bounce — an adjustment that makes it possible for her to continue to play the game and enjoy its aerobic benefits.

ILL HEALTH AND DEPENDENCY

We have already noted the ambivalent attitudes of our respondents concerning retirement centers and nursing homes as places to spend their last years. Nevertheless, many of these surviving lesbians, especially those alone or lacking family support or both, need to consider who will care for them in the event of a serious illness or a severe disability that makes it impossible for them to care for themselves. The majority (60) would opt for help from a partner, friend, or neighbor. If these were not available, 34 feel they could still make a claim on a family member. The third choice (for 21) would be a health professional (presumably an MSW) or referral to a social/health agency. Twenty-nine checked "don't know." For severe emotional health problems, 72 would seek help first from a mental health professional, a religious counselor, or a physician. The next preference (for 52) would be to call upon their lover, partner, or a friend. Again, only if these were not available or were unwilling to assume the responsibility, the choice (of 15) would be a family member. Two checked "don't know."

We cannot help but notice the relatively low priority given to family members, whether because there aren't any or because, if they exist, they would not be supportive. In either case, it becomes apparent that many lesbians in their advanced years will need care in a sympathetic environment where they will not have to disguise their background and life-style. Fortunately, several efforts are being made to establish such facilities for both gay men and lesbians. A recent survey (1986) of the retirement housing preference of 456 homosexuals over 55 (57% of them female), made by A. J. Lucco, MD, of the Levindale Geriatric Center in Baltimore, yielded some valuable data for those involved in the planning stages of such facilities.

For example, Galaxy, a San Francisco-based group, is working in connection with the Unitarian Church to organize shared housing for lesbian and gay elders in the Bay Area, with the intention of expanding to health care facilities later. Another fund-raising venture to establish "a place of our own" for lesbians in New York City has been undertaken by Matrix, an organization whose vision includes permanent housing for older lesbians. It is the hope of its originator, Chris Almvig, cofounder of Senior Action in a Gay Environment (SAGE), that Matrix will provide intergenerational accommodation, combining a "holistic health and fitness center" with other services for "our older sisters." Meanwhile, other communities have inaugurated programs of shared housing for gay male and female elders so that, by the turn of the century, we should have not only our own retirement centers, but our own convalescent and nursing homes, at least in the larger metropolitan areas, a welcome prospect to those of us presently in the 60-plus category.

For those in need now, one alternative currently available is a volunteer program made up of younger lesbians who visit and assist their older sisters temporarily hospitalized or bedridden at home. The group Gay and Lesbian Outreach to Elders (GLOE) in San Francisco is a good example of such intergenerational collaboration already underway. Known as "friendly visitors," the volunteers are in touch by telephone and regularly visit those members who are incapacitated. They also serve as a link to other social service organizations that provide further care. In addition, some volunteers assist with clerical work in the GLOE office and participate in speaking engagements to further the understanding of the organization and its work.[2]

EMOTIONAL HEALTH

It is perhaps to be expected that the relatively select population of physically healthy older women studied here would also be emotionally healthy but for the pressures created by their deviant lifestyles. Even with the hazards of being gay, they have somehow maintained their emotional balance, with 82 rating themselves in "excellent" or "good" emotional health. One of those now in "excellent" shape narrated her experience as follows:

> I guess I've always known I was a lesbian. Because I learned early that lesbianism was a sickness, I went for therapy at age 28 to get "cured" of it. Treatment was successful to the extent that I avoided any situation that might hint of it. Even in the service I didn't see any lesbianism (during World War II). When I retired at age 55 to a lesbian/gay community in the West, I came out with a vengeance. Since then I've had the happiest years of my life. I feel I finally belong somewhere.

Seventeen others have been in therapy for their sexual preference at some time in the past. At the time of the survey, only one was in group therapy for adjustment to her lesbianism.

In view of the discrimination that many of these women have experienced — in employment, in their own families (as children and as parents), in their social life (from younger lesbians as well as from heterosexuals), it is surely remarkable that they have been strong enough to survive with so little emotional support available. Some of those who were brought up as Catholics (before there was a supportive Dignity organization) endured severe religious conflicts. One, widowed from a relationship with a woman, wrote that she continues to be torn:

> At this writing I have an appointment with a psychologist. I have had some, albeit rare, suicidal thoughts. I find myself rationalizing the intent as a decision with no feeling of consequence to others, or myself, concerning a religious aspect.

Another, who has felt religious discrimination in the past, responded to the question (No. 63) on the source of discrimination by writing, "The Catholic Church and its attitude toward homosexuals, though now, in many local parishes, large steps are being taken to recognize that we are a part of the Church community." In reference to her lifelong religious struggle, the same woman recounted:

> When I finally matured enough to do a lot of reading about homosexuality and the Church, talked to nuns, priests, and friends about it, then did some praying and talking to myself, I was able to become comfortable being a lesbian and having

sexual relations with my partner. The Dignity organization is a welcome resource and fills many needs for *all* ages of homosexual Catholics.

Yet these women, along with their nongay peers, also know discrimination because of their age, even from those in their own lesbian community. One attempted to explain it by writing, "Almost all known younger lesbians feel they will become aged and do not want to face it." Others expressed their disappointment differently: "I would like to see younger women working to change negative images of old age among other young women and more effort given to older women running older women's programs"; "Younger lesbians talk a good one how bad ageism is, but *socially* they want nothing to do with older women"; "There is a degree of ageism in the lesbian community here—a certain amount of patronizing." One woman summed it up: "The lesbian community thinks young."

Neither ageism nor the scars of discrimination distress these women as much as loneliness, which still seems to be the most serious emotional problem for lesbians in their sixth decade and beyond. Regrettably, we neglected to include in our research any questions on how many and what kinds of pets our respondents had. A growing body of literature testifies to the value of pet therapy for those in institutional settings such as prisons, nursing homes, and so on, while less has been done until recently to examine the social impact of pets on the health of individuals. In the 1980s, experimental studies have investigated the effects of pet ownership on coronary recovery and blood pressure. The results show significant benefits from the human-animal interaction. One finding was that blood pressure increases when people talk to people, but decreases when they talk to animals. Since hypertension was the second most common ailment mentioned by our respondents, the human-animal interaction may be of some concern to them. In return for the nurturance and affection they elicit, pets reward the owner with uncritical acceptance and devotion. A kind of symbiotic relationship develops, and the tactile deprivation that often accompanies loneliness in both animal and human societies is lessened. For those living alone, pets can be "someone" to come home to, instead of an empty house or apartment.[3]

ATTITUDES TOWARD LESBIANISM AND AGING

Gerontologists tell us that most old people are in good mental health, and most psychologists would agree that a good self-image is an important part of successful adaptation to old age. The large majority (71) of our respondents to the question (No. 62), "How do you feel about being a lesbian?" answered "very positive." But, in reply to a similar question (No. 64) about aging, only 24 were "very positive." The same number checked "somewhat nega- tive," while the largest number (27) were "somewhat positive" in their attitude toward growing old. One, just on the threshold of 60 at the time of this survey, voiced the common complaint, "As I get older, life gets lonelier and more fearful. One becomes less sure of herself and wonders where and how life will end." Another had no problems except for "getting older and older." Our subjects seem to have weathered the widely held view that homosexuality is an illness better than they have been able to withstand the feeling of invalidation that accompanies aging. As one woman wrote, "What can I do? I'd like to be 35 forever. No younger, no older. But I'm aging." She then tempered her dejection with the thought, "If I've got my health, it's O.K."

Although it was not until the 1970s that androgyny became a popular subject for psychological research, and studies found greater self-esteem among those who participated in both social sex roles,[4] most of the lesbians over 60 who have never been married to a man developed a conception of themselves as strong and indepen- dent individuals. Relying on no one, they value courage, assertive- ness, and determination, personality characteristics usually associ- ated with masculinity. Their careers and financial provision for their old age have also had to be important components of their value systems. Because of their androgynous makeup, they tend to deny the onset of the frailty that inevitably accompanies advanced age. Those alone and without family support, or those who may lack confidence in what they view as a macho medical system intent on discarding the elderly, may postpone seeking needed professional health care. Sometimes this avoidance or delay, especially on the occasion of a serious illness, can result in complications and greater disability.

As more clinics for women (staffed by women) are established with female geriatric specialists, much of the hesitation of these lesbians to seek help may be overcome in time. The future of the gerontological nursing practice may also benefit from greater sensitivity to the needs of elderly patients, both female and male, who have led an alternative life-style. In order to achieve such understanding, it may be desirable to offer more courses in "Lesbian and Gay Aging" in university gerontology programs, where care providers often get their basic training.[5]

NOTES

1. One of his subjects was over 60.

2. Gay and Lesbian Outreach to Elders (GLOE) has a complement of young men who offer equivalent services for elderly males in comparable circumstances. They also serve the organization in similar capacities as those described for the women volunteers.

3. This information was derived from conversations with Christine M. Shaheen, Director of the San Francisco SPCA Animal-assisted Therapy Program, in which the author participates as a volunteer. This program is only one of the many services developed by the San Francisco SPCA for the elderly, especially those on low fixed incomes. As a volunteer visiting nursing and convalescent homes, as well as adult day-care centers (in most of which women outnumber men 5 to 1), I have observed how a woman's eyes light up when she has a furry animal that she can cuddle in her lap even for a few moments. (The men, in their macho tradition, usually ignore the pet — unless it's a chicken or a turtle. Then they joke with some remark such as "I'll take the white meat," or "Soup's on!") Although many institutions for the elderly (including board and care homes) have a house cat, rabbit, or bird, individual residents cannot, as a rule, keep private pets; thus, the bonding between human and animal, which can relieve so much loneliness, is not possible.

For those alone and still able to live independently, as so many of the women in our study do, pets can lessen the feelings of isolation and boredom. They can help reshape lives crumbled by retirement or personal loss. In my own case, my 16-year-old dog and cat, with me since they were babies, are my constant companions, and their demands keep me often amused and always aware of the schedule I must keep.

In 1987, the San Francisco SPCA extended its Animal-assisted Therapy Program to AIDS patients of all ages.

For more on this topic, see my article, "Loneliness and the Elderly Homosexual: Is Pet Therapy the Answer?" in the *Journal of Homosexuality*'s forthcoming special issue on aging.

4. For a full treatment of this topic, see Larson, P. C. (1981). Sexual identity and self-concept. *Journal of Homosexuality*, 7(1), 15-32.

5. For a description of the first such course, given at San Francisco State University (by the author) in the summer of 1986, see the Appendix.

Chapter 6

Lesbians and Gay
Men Over 60

DIFFICULTIES OF COMPARISON:
THE BERGER AND KEHOE STUDIES

A comparison (or contrast) of females and males in our sexist society is usually expected of investigators of either group, but such an attempt is difficult if not impossible in the case of the population under study here. There is relatively little information specifically on gay males over 60 because few researchers have focused exclusively on them or, when they have, the numbers or scope of the investigations have been so limited as to make the results inconclusive.

In Dr. Raymond Berger's *Gay and Gray* (G&G), the most extensive survey of older gay men to date,[1] "older" meant *over 40*. Thirty percent of his 112 subjects were over 60; these elder "olders" were not treated separately. The ages of the 10 men Berger interviewed were described as "from 44 to 72" (p. 21). He mentioned age in connection with his interviewees only rarely, as on page 22 when he referred to two of them "in their seventies who had chronic health problems associated with advanced age."

Of course, much of what the literature on homosexuality — mostly by males about males[2] — claims for the "older" gay man applies as well, and maybe in some cases more so, to the "aging" gay woman. ("Aging" is another of those terms that need definition because we are all "aging" at any age.) For example, "the invisibility of older homosexuals within the gay community," which Berger mentioned in his Introduction (p. 14), is surely shared by lesbians over 60, who are less likely to frequent the women's bars or participate in public events such as the Gay Freedom Day Parade[3] than their younger cohorts. Needless to say, they do not generally patronize bathhouses, although one in San Francisco did have a "ladies" night.[4] Another point made in *Gay and Gray*, that "older homosexuals are isolated from each other" (p. 14), certainly applies to most of those lesbians who are retired and living outside metropolitan areas, where organizations such as SAGE in New York and GLOE in San Francisco bring them together.

Curiously, there seem to be fewer stereotypes of lesbians over 60 than there are for older homosexual males. Perhaps this is due to the greater invisibility of the women and to the fact that they are triply disregarded: as female, as aged, and as deviant. If they are thought of at all by the heterosexual public at large, it is as pathetic, freakish figures, rejected by their families and hiding out of shame.

DIFFERENCE IN METHOD

There are considerable differences in the method of the Berger and Kehoe studies. Berger incorporated interviews with 10 individuals of unspecified ages, a salient part of his book. Limited funding prevented us from being able to conduct personal interviews as part of our research. The purposes of the two studies were also rather different. Our principal effort was simply to gather data,[5] rather than to "refute stereotypes" or "identify factors which predict successful adaptation to aging" for the population surveyed (Berger, p. 123). Also, our sample was nationwide, encompassing all regions of the continental United States, while the sample in *Gay and Gray* was from a "four-county area" in "one locale" (Berger, p. 123-124).[6]

The questionnaires used in both surveys covered comparable areas of inquiry, although, of course, with different wording and different organization of cluster items. Like the sample in *Gay and Gray*, ours (we may even quote) "does not purport to represent all" lesbian women over 60, "and the results presented here do not provide a statistical profile of this group" (Berger, p. 123). Like the Berger team, we had great difficulty recruiting nonwhites, with only 6% of our respondents falling outside the category of white. However, this is more to be expected with women, considering the greater conservatism ascribed to them and the traditional attachment of minority women to family, an inherited value system, or religion.[7]

"In defense of the appropriateness of the sample" again, in both Berger and Kehoe, "nearly all respondents were strongly self-identified as homosexual" (Berger, p. 124). As with *Gay and Gray*, we can make "several observations . . . in defense of the diversity of our sample" (Berger, p. 123). *Lesbians Over Sixty* (LOS) included representatives of both the "young-old" (60 to 75) and the "old-old" (75 to 86), various levels of education, income, and a variety of occupations, retirement statuses, and religious/spiritual identifications.[8] As for our recruitment of minorities, we were not very successful, either. We were able to attract only one American Indian, two Asians, and one Black, but no Hispanic participants. Two respondents wrote in "Jewish" under the ethnic question (No. 75), but did not circle "Jewish" under the religious identification (No. 76). One said she was of mixed parentage, half European and half American Indian, and one skipped the question (No. 75) altogether.

At first glance, it would seem that the scales on sexual behavior (Table 2 in *Gay and Gray*, p. 128, and Table 12 in the Appendix, Preliminary Report, to *Lesbians Over Sixty*) might be compared, but even allowing for the age difference of the subjects, other more serious discrepancies in the ratings exist. We asked for information on sexual *history*, rather than on self-perception of sexual *orientation*, with different wording and a reversal of the order of the scale. A juxtaposition of the two shows the difficulty of attempting such a comparison. (See Table 1.)

Trying to deduce parallels from matching any of the other tables always presents the age incompatibility of subjects, as well as other differences in intent and wording. However, many of the general comments made, in passim, by Berger do have some relevance to our research informants. In his observations on bisexuality (p. 128), he noted that since the 1960s "the opening up of traditionally male sports and occupations to women" has promoted a certain tolerance for "sexual ambiguity." This trend has undoubtedly made it easier for those lesbians now over 60, who were late bloomers, to adjust more comfortably to an alternative life-style.

Table 1

Comparison of Berger and Kehoe Sexual Behavior Scales

Exclusively homosexual	86.6%	Exclusively heterosexual	0%
Primarily homosexual, only slightly heterosexual	11.6%	Largely heterosexual, but with incidental homosexual history	6%
Primarily homosexual, but more than slightly heterosexual	1.8%	Largely heterosexual, but with distinct homosexual history	14%
Equally homosexual and heterosexual	0%	Equally heterosexual and homosexual	5%
Primarily heterosexual, but more than slightly homosexual	0%	Largely homosexual, but with distinct heterosexual history	12%
Primarily heterosexual, only slightly homosexual	0%	Largely homosexual, but with incidental heterosexual history	23%
Exclusively heterosexual	0%	Exclusively homosexual	39%
		Without either homosexual or heterosexual history	1%

DIFFERENCE IN SUBJECTS' LIVING SITUATIONS

Under "Living Situation," the author of *Gay and Gray* mentioned that "For the older homosexual man who is likely to frequent public gay institutions (bars, clubs, and other social/sexual outlets) less frequently, the home is an especially important source of social and emotional support" (p. 130). This, of course, is even more true for the lesbian over 60, whose social life is more likely to involve private small-group gatherings in homes, rather than larger, more impersonal meetings in public places. If she is retired and living alone (57% of our respondents are and do), home may be an even more important sanctuary.

DIFFERENCE IN MARITAL STATUS

When one considers marital status, it is not surprising that a much larger percentage (42%) of the women in the LOS survey, than the men (29%) in the G&G study, had been in a conventional male-female marriage. As we have said, being more conservative and, for the most part, growing up in a less sexually liberated era than most of the men, the women would be more likely to conform to the traditional life-style. They were of marriageable age in the 1930s and 1940s when, as Berger pointed out, "social pressures to marry were much greater than they are today" (p. 131), so it is no wonder that more of them capitulated. Also, more of the women, who we have called late bloomers, were unaware of their affectional/sexual preference, or the possibility of an alternate life-style, until midlife or later.

DIFFERENCE IN EDUCATIONAL BACKGROUND

It is, on the other hand, surprising that more than twice as many of our lesbian respondents (47%) have advanced degrees as compared with Berger's respondents (21.8%). This is particularly remarkable in view of the greater opportunity, before the middle of this century, for males to pursue graduate education. Perhaps our method of recruitment — in particular, that done through Women's Studies programs and announcements in academic journals — was responsible for eliciting responses from the well educated section of the 60-plus lesbian population. Berger, who reported that he "placed advertisements and articles in local gay publications . . . distributed to gay bars and clubs" (p. 121) would presumably draw quite a different group of respondents. Again, and probably for the same reasons as mentioned above, we drew participants from the higher occupational levels, with 70% in professional categories, while the male study had 21.7% in "executive or professional occupations. Twenty-five percent of the men were retired (not quite equaling the 30% of them over 60 years of age), while 59% of our women had chosen to stop working.

DIFFERENCE IN INCOMES

Comparing incomes, as of 1978 for G&G and 1984 for LOS, with different high and low amounts shows, once more, the difficulty of attempting such comparative analyses. For the G&G sample, 35.5% had incomes of over $18,000, while 60% of the LOS sample had incomes of over $15,000. For the G&G sample, 10.9% had incomes of less than $6,000, while 3% of the LOS sample had incomes of less than $5,000.

In regard to their health, about the same number of men (86.6%), with 70% of them *under* 60 years of age, reported good or excellent health. A similar number, 82%, of the 60-plus women reported the same. For whatever reasons, lesbians are survivors.

The next section in Berger's chapter, "What Are Older Homosexual Men Like," explored the psychological and social adaptation of the subjects. It began with a review of some of the earlier studies on homosexuality and mentioned their preoccupation with heterosexual-homosexual comparisons to show that gays are "just as good." The author also called our attention to the "causality trap" as descriptive of some of the earlier investigations, many of them having been obsessed with etiology. LOS, like G&G, differed from most of these in that it attempted only to find out what the aged lesbian is like, not to inquire into the origin of her behavior or make judgments about its value.

DIFFERENCE IN PSYCHOLOGICAL AND SOCIAL ADAPTATION

Among the measures that G&G employed to examine the older homosexual man's psychological and social adaptation (p. 140), we, too, used the following:

1. *Self-acceptance.* For Question No. 62, "How do you feel about being a lesbian?" 71% checked "very positive," and for Question No. 64, "How do you feel about your own aging?" 51% checked "very" or "somewhat positive." These results compare

favorably with those items in G&G that deal with the same concerns but with very different scales and questions. Berger's respondents scored high (82.1%) "for self-acceptance" (p. 142) and did "not show any unusual preoccupation with aging" (p. 148).

2. *Life Satisfaction*. For Question No. 60, the scores on the scale used indicate that the great majority rated high (38%) or medium (48%) in life satisfaction. This speaks well of the 60-plus women, more advanced in years than G&G's men, who also rated high on a comparable scale.

3. *Fears and Anxieties*. For Question No. 62, "How do you feel about being a lesbian?" (see No. 1 above), 71% of our gay women indicated full acceptance of their identity as lesbians and otherwise expressed little anxiety about their life-style. As aged persons, many of whom became lesbians late in life after long heterosexual relationships, they would have given careful consideration to the risks involved. Some of them, in the beginning, may only have been seeking out a supportive women's community, having been influenced by the women's movement of the 1960s and 1970s. Those retired would no longer be anxious about damaging their careers or losing their jobs. Then, too, they would have been more likely to have achieved some financial stability in their late maturity, either in a divorce settlement, as widows, or, if they had remained single, by means of their own savings. Likewise, about the same proportion of men in G&G had also overcome the feelings of guilt and shame that some of their younger counterparts may suffer.

The attitude of the lesbians toward aging was one of relative acceptance, with 51% feeling positive about it, and only 5% very negative. In response to the question, "Do you worry about growing old?" Berger's respondents admitted they did, either sometimes (41.4%) or often (9%). Considering not only the difference in age of the two groups, but also the reputed greater importance of youth in the gay male culture, it is surprising that more of the men surveyed did not indicate more concern about aging. On the other hand, our late bloomers may have been more affected by the "beauty culture" demands of their former heterosexual life-style.

4. *Counseling Experience*. As an index of psychological and social adaptation, counseling experience is, according to Berger, a poor indicator of psychological health because "there is no clear

relationship between an individual's seeking out counseling and his psychological health" (p. 150). Besides this, the individual may be trying to resolve some problem in a relationship, rather than in connection with homosexual behavior itself or its "cure." And, of course, to seek out psychiatric help in "the old days" was tantamount to an admission of lunacy. Furthermore, the questions asked in both studies do not inquire at what age the individuals had the experience. There is also the possibility that some respondents might be unwilling to admit having been in therapy.

With all of these misgivings, and the differences in subjects, wording, and intent, the results of the parallel questions were as follows:

Gay and Gray

In the past have you ever received counseling from a mental health professional such as a psychiatrist, psychologist, social worker, or counselor?

Yes: 28.9%
No: 71.2%

Are you presently receiving such counseling?

Yes: 1.8%
No: 98.2%

Lesbians Over Sixty

Have you ever been in therapy concerning your lesbianism?

Yes: 18%
No: 80% (2 unreported)

(If yes) Are you presently in therapy for this same reason?

Yes: 1%
No: 17%

The lesbian presently in therapy added the word "group" after her answer, which, unfortunately, does not tell us its purpose. Another who answered "yes" to the first part of the question added "only between 6 and 9 years of age and not by choice." How many others may have had involuntary counseling as a child, we do not know.

The entire counseling question clearly needs to be handled by interview.

5. *Passing*. Passing, concealment or being closeted, has usually been less of a concern for lesbians than for gay men. Historically, female sexuality has been trivialized along with children's sandbox explorations of each other. For males to degrade themselves into passive femininity by sodomy has been the main focus of the law. The famous tale of Queen Victoria's veto of the inclusion of women in the 19th-century British antisodomy laws, because *they didn't do such dreadful things*, is an indication of the popular view of the period. Romantic attachments between women were considered just expressions of their inherent gushy sentimentality. Society in the first half of the 20th century continued to view lesbianism, at least legally, in this somewhat more indulgent manner. After all, what can two women do together? However, Lillian Faderman pointed out that "(until the lesbian-feminist movement) 20th century women were largely forced to deny their love for other women" because of the morbidification of intense love relationships between women by late 19th-century medical science and psychology — the "queer" or "sick" syndrome.[9]

In such an environment, those who aspired to professional careers had to conceal their deviant behavior from most of their co-workers. Many women in the LOS study had been homemakers, so almost a fourth skipped the question on coming out to co-workers as not applicable, whereas in G&G (Table 21, p. 156), only 5.7% checked N.A. (not applicable). Although the question was not asked in G&G, more than half (52%) of the women in LOS had not come out to neighbors. This, again, underscores the importance lesbians place on keeping their home a private place, a refuge from public scrutiny.

As Berger concluded from his investigation of older men, "the older homosexual may be less concerned with exposure" (p. 157). This is apparently equally true of lesbians. Those in LOS were "out" to 95% of their friends, of whom 63% were homosexual, and to 68% of their family members. Some of our 60-plus lesbians never told their parents, most of whom are deceased, but find it less difficult to reveal their homoerotic preference to their adult children who have grown up in a more liberated era.

6. *"Relationship to Younger Age Cohorts."* The two pertinent

questions in the LOS survey (Nos. 30 and 36), focused specifically on "partner" relationships, whereas G&G included both homo- and heterosexual associations. In the latter, the research showed that "there was a marked preference for socializing with same age peers" (G&G, p. 158). In response to the LOS question that asked the respondents' preference for partners (No. 36), the results indicate that the majority (64%) also preferred socializing with same-age peers. Apropos G&G's definition of an age peer as "any individual within ten years of the respondent's age or older" (p. 158), we may note that none of the women preferred anyone "more than 10 years older" and 31% had "no preference."

According to our inquiry, old lesbians seem to have less expectation or experience of negative attitudes from their younger cohorts than do the more diverse age group of men in G&G. Berger suggested that, for gay males, "negative attitudes on the part of both generations lead to mutual avoidance" (p. 160). Seventy-four percent of the women reported never having felt any discrimination from other lesbians because of their age (Question No. 66). In our discussions at Gay and Lesbian Outreach to Elders of plans for a retirement community for lesbians, I have noticed how most of the women involved are very antipathetic toward the idea of a home exclusively for old lesbians. They would prefer an intergenerational facility where accommodations would be available for age 40-plus residents as well as 60-plus residents. Because the physical aspects of the relationship often grow less important for gay women as they grow older, while the need for warmth, affection, emotional support, dependability, and companionship increases, aging is not so critical a barrier.

7. *Sex Life*. We would expect the sex life of the men over 40 in G&G to be considerably more active than that of the women in LOS at 60 and beyond. Allowing for the difference in the time span covered (6 months in G&G and one year in LOS) and the frequency breakdown, the contrast is clear, as shown below:

Gay and Gray

Average frequency of same sex-relations over the past 6 months:
3 times or more a week. 18.9%
More than once, up to twice a week. 27.9%

About once a week. 14.4%
More than once a week
   but less than 4 times a month. 18.0%
Once a month 14.4%
Never. 6.3%

Lesbians Over Sixty

Over the last year, how often were you physically sexual with another woman?

Daily. 3.0%
About once a week. 15.0%
About once a month. 8.0%
A few times a year. 16.0%
Never. 53.0%

The most significant difference is in the "Never" category. However, in the case of the lesbians, celibacy is not always voluntary. Seventy-four percent of those who are currently celibate (34 of the total) indicated that their situation was not by choice. Therefore, we may presume they would be more active sexually if they had the opportunity. Their dissatisfaction was revealed to some extent in the question (No. 41), "How satisfied have you been with your sex life over the last year?" which is compared below with the same G&G question, but again for a shorter (6-month) period:

Gay and Gray (6 months)

Very satisfied. 21.4%
Satisfied. 25.9%
Somewhat satisfied. 25.9%
Unsatisfied. 16.1%
Very unsatisfied. 10.7%

Lesbians Over Sixty (one year)

Very satisfied. 16%
Somewhat satisfied. 17%
Neither satisfied nor unsatisfied. 20%
Somewhat unsatisfied. 21%
Very unsatisfied. 26%

In our older female sample, it appears that more subjects would find greater satisfaction if sex partners were available. In reference to lesbians of the over-60 generation, this means more opportunities for socializing because for them, friendship is an almost necessary precursor to more intimate relationships. The increased cautiousness of older people that Berger wrote about (p. 164) also operates, presumably to an even greater extent, to inhibit women of advanced age in this type of risk-taking.

Sex is not the main part of a relationship for any of our respondents, and an unimportant part for 28%, while 78% have a positive attitude toward monogamy (as reported in Question No. 45). Thus, it is inevitable that their interest and participation in sexual activity should be quite different, and probably less, than that of their male counterparts. Unfortunately, we do not have comparable data on homosexual males in the 60-plus age bracket, so we cannot be specific about the difference. Such a study should be forthcoming soon, however. With the growing concern for the aging, gay gerontologists will surely be encouraged to investigate this special population.

NOTES

1. For a review of the research on older gay men, see the introduction and bibliography in Berger's 1982 book, *Gay and Gray*, University of Illinois Press, Urbana, IL.

2. The first issue of the *Journal of Homosexuality* devoted entirely to the topic of lesbianism appeared in 1986 with the author, Dr. Kehoe, as guest editor.

3. In San Francisco, the Gay and Lesbian Outreach to Elders (GLOE) provides motorized cable cars for its over-60 members so they can ride in the parade, but only a few of the lesbians, the regulars who attend everything, usually show up.

4. The bath houses have been closed as a result of the AIDS epidemic.

5. Our purposes are outlined in detail in Chapter 1.

6. This comparison is certainly not intended to disparage the very thorough and substantial Berger research, but only to indicate one of the differences.

7. It may be of some interest to note how, in San Francisco, the young Asian and Hispanic lesbians seem to be coming out more than those in their parents' generation. They have their own gathering places, including a preferred women's bar.

8. See the tables in the Appendix (Preliminary Report).

9. Faderman, L. (1978). The morbidification of love between women by 19th-century sexologists. *Journal of Homosexuality, 4,* 73.

Conclusion

A Profile of the 60-Plus Lesbian of This Study

Our subject is white, 67 years of age, and overweight. She was born in a middle western urban area, but now lives on the Pacific coast, alone, in her own home. She has never been married to a man and is childless. She has no known gay relatives. Her religious identification is Protestant, and she is a registered Democrat. Her education and work experience are above average and place her in the professional category. She holds a graduate degree and is now retired. Her gross income in 1983 was between $25,000 and $50,000 a year.

She does not smoke and is a social drinker only. She exercises regularly and prefers concerts and the theater to any other entertainment. She loves to travel and spends much of her free time reading. She does not frequent bars, lesbian or otherwise, but does belong to a lesbian social group, and most of her friends are lesbians. She does not use the mainline senior centers and would prefer a "lesbian only" retirement community.

Her self-image is good and she feels very positive about being a lesbian. She has not been aware of being discriminated against because of her life-style. She has adjusted to her own aging, but has suffered some discrimination from both heterosexuals and homosexuals because of it.

She is not currently involved with another woman and has always considered sex only "one important part" of any relationship. Her female partner has usually been within 10 years of her own age, and none has been more than 10 years older. She believes in monogamy and has never wanted to change her sex. Her history indicates that she has been either exclusively homosexual, or homosexual with only incidental heterosexual episodes. She is not bisexual and has not been involved in heterosexual role playing. Her experience of relationships in her earlier life has been one of serial monogamy.

In spite of minor attacks of arthritis and some hypertension, her physical and emotional health are either "excellent" or "good." She has never been in therapy because of her lesbianism. Although she has occasional bouts with loneliness, she seems able to cope with it, as she does with the minor physical afflictions she endures as she ages.

It must be noted that this profile of a well-adjusted elder, constructed from the majority of responses to our questionnaire, applies to no one individual, nor is it a stereotype. It in no way diminishes the real problems of the nearly two million lesbians over 60 in the United States not reached by this survey who may not have the advantages of our respondents. Those who may be ill, economically deprived, institutionalized, or living with unsympathetic relatives are probably in the majority. Their living conditions will not improve until society becomes more accepting of their subcultural diversity.

SUMMARY

With all its faults, this study, begun in 1983, is the first attempt to reach a nationwide representation of lesbian elders in order to gather information about their background, their relationship with their families of origin, and, for those married to men, with their husbands, children, and grandchildren. It explores their sexual behavior, both their physical and psychological health, and how aging has affected them. With the relatively meagre data available, it tries to make some comparison between lesbians and gay men over 60. All of this is just a beginning, an effort, it is hoped, that will encourage researchers to investigate further this hidden population that is another fascinating component of our diverse society.

Through our research, we established that gay women of advanced age, as we have long surmised, are everywhere. Like their younger cohorts, they live in all regions of America, rural as well as urban. They come in all colors and are from all occupations: professional, business, clerical, trades, domestic work, and land management, to name a few. Many of them are now retired. Their formal education ranges from high school diplomas to doctorate degrees. A few are financially well off, while another few live below the poverty line. The rest enjoy reasonable comfort in their own homes, on modest incomes. In both political and religious affiliation, they tend to be liberal.

Their sexual history runs the gamut from exclusively homosexual, through equally homosexual and heterosexual, to asexual. As they age and sex becomes a less significant part of their relationships, companionship grows more important. They prefer to associate with other lesbians within 10 years of their own age, whom they meet in community social groups, through friends, or at work — but not in bars. They do not relish the thought of ending their lives in any institution for the aged, but would consider a gay/lesbian intergenerational retirement community acceptable.

Their most serious problems, even with the advantaged group surveyed, are those that affect many women of advanced age in our society: loneliness and economic worries. Although the feminization of poverty has been a topic under public scrutiny for some time, because it involves women of all ages, less attention has been paid to it in relation to the elderly. The equally disabling condition brought on by their isolation and loneliness has also been disregarded. In spite of the fact that lesbians should find it easier than heterosexual women do to share their lives with each other, it grows increasingly difficult the older they get. They often lack the energy required to begin again in a new relationship, with all the adjustment and accommodation necessary to live with even a compatible person.

Those who married and came to lesbianism late in life reported that they have kept in closer contact with their female relatives (mother, sister, daughter, granddaughter) and received more support from them than from the males in their families. In spite of their advanced years, their physical and emotional health is good, and they score in the upper percentiles on the Life Satisfaction Scale. The large majority feel positive about their life-style and even about aging. This outlook manifests a well-being that puts these women in a rather special category.

I salute the women who participated in this study, along with all those others out there, many less fortunate, who have, as an endangered species, resisted the coercive force of heterosexual ideology and lived their long lives in allegiance to their own perceived identity.

Appendix

Gerontology/
Applied
Certificate
Program offers...

Lesbian and Gay Aging [1]

Designed to familiarize students with special
problems of aging lesbians and gay males. This
course reviews the literature on aging homosexuals,
and lesbians and the community resources established
to deal with their needs. Social attitudes toward
sexual deviance and the nature of homophobia is
considered. An examination of the results of the
Berger and Kehoe studies include full descriptions
of this relatively invisible segment of society and
its adaptation to aging.

Instructor:
Monika Kehoe, Ph.D., Research Associate, Center
for Education and Research in Sexuality, SFSU;
author, lecturer and scholar in lesbian and gay issues.

Dates/Location:
Friday, March 6, 6-9 pm; Saturdays, March 7, 14,
21, 28, 3-6 pm, SFSU, Education Building, Room 301.

Fee: $75.
Call #469-1684, for more information.

SAN FRANCISCO STATE UNIVERSITY
GERONTOLOGY PROGRAMS
20 Tapia Drive • San Francisco 94132

SAN FRANCISCO STATE UNIVERSITY EXTENDED EDUCATION

EVALUATION:
LESBIANS OVER SIXTY
A NATIONAL SURVEY

1. The project formulated its sample size following budget changes during the pre-funding stage. Sample size was reduced from 150 to 100 individuals. Distribution of instruments began February 1984. At the closing date of July 1, 1984, 134 instruments had been distributed. Two were received too late and one potential respondent was fifty-nine years of age. One hundred instruments were utilized for analysis.

Recall that respondents were identified by word of mouth, and flyers to resources within the aging, women's and gay communities. Hundreds of flyers and press releases were distributed. Later, staff will report on how respondents actually found out about the survey. The Project and Research Coordinators, both lesbian researchers, were able to make personal contact with potential respondents.

Face to face contacts were initiated only during the pilot testing phase at the Gay and Lesbian Outreach to Elders Program — Social Service Component of Operation Concern, San Francisco.

Again, during the budgetary reformulation stage, the decision was made to eliminate face to face and telephone assessments.

To date all 100 instruments have been received, coded and summarized using the Statistical Package for the Social Sciences

---

Published findings of Lesbians Over Sixty: A National Survey available from Anabel O. Pelham or Sheryl Goldberg.

(SPSS). San Francisco State University computers have been utilized for this task.

Frequencies for all questions have been reported and cross tabulation (chi square) statistics have been determined for 30 tested hypotheses. Percentages for all appropriate questions have been determined and summaries for all open-ended questions are being written in narrative form (see final report).

Interpretations of findings are being written in several forms: this final report; articles for scientific journals; papers for presentation at scientific meetings, for example, Western Gerontological Society; presentation in scientific meeting panels, for example, the National Council on Aging; and publication for the gay and lesbian community and community-at-large.

Additionally, copies of findings will be distributed to sixty-six respondents who requested final analyses. Findings will be distributed to the same agencies who originally assisted in locating respondents across the United States. There are thirty of these community agencies.

Finally, action steps under each project objective were completed within the time frame originally created. All tasks were created on time and within budget.

We are impressed by the fact that the project was able to locate 100 elder participants in such an efficient, timely fashion. Also impressive are the facts that 9 percent of the participants are seventy-five years of age and older and 17 percent report a physical problem or illness that seriously affects health or restricts activity. Overall we are pleased with the quality of this survey research and contribution to the field of Gerontology.

CERES   • *Center for Research and Education in Sexuality*

San Francisco State University

Psychology Building Room 502   •   (415) 469-1137
1600 Holloway Avenue   •   San Francisco, California 94132

LESBIANS-OVER-60: A NATIONAL SURVEY

John P. DeCecco, Ph.D., Project Director
Monika Kehoe, Ph.D., Project Coordinator
Sheryl Goldberg, MSW, Research Coordinator

PRELIMINARY REPORT
OCTOBER 1984

The 1984 nationwide study of lesbians over 60, conducted under the auspices of CERES (Center for Research and Education in Sexuality) at San Francisco State University, has been completed, the results computerized for analysis, and the findings summarized herewith.

Although questionnaires from more than one hundred participants were received, the survey was limited to the first hundred. These respondents are women aged 60 to 86, living in all sections of the continental U.S. and reared in urban, rural, suburban, and small town settings (Tables 1, 2, 3). The majority are well-educated with almost half (47%) having advanced degrees (Table 4). More than half (57%) presently live alone in a single dwelling which they own (Tables 5, 6). They are primarily caucasian (94%) and financially comfortable (Tables 7, 8). The majority are registered politically as democrats and are affiliated with a Christian religious denomination or "none" (Tables 9, 10). Close to 75% have worked as professionals when employed. Almost a third (32%) are still employed (Table 11). Of those who served in the military (27%), only one was discharged because of lesbianism. (Since a random sample of a hidden population is impossible to collect, our group may be somewhat homogenous.)

As self-identified lesbians (Table 12), they acknowledge that most of their friends are women, often younger lesbians (Tables 13,

14). They meet friends in social gatherings or through other friends, not in bars (Table 15). Indeed, this lesbian, as represented in our survey, does not frequent bars.

Only 5% regularly participate in senior center programs or use their services. The majority express a preference for either exclusively lesbian or lesbian/gay-only retirement communities, nursing homes, and/or social organizations (Table 16). This points up the need for such facilities where elderly lesbians and gays can feel "at home" with those who understand them and have shared their lifestyle.

In spite of the fact that the majority seem to be free of serious problems, loneliness tops all others as the one most often mentioned. Perhaps, as a result of family strain, few respondents have close kin connections. When they do, they appear to be predominantly with female relatives (Table 17). Also, it may be of some significance that only 12% report themselves as the only child, contrary to some expectations (Table 18). More friends than family members are aware of their lesbianism (Table 19). Also, of the 30% who reported having lesbian or gay relatives, a fourth of these were the women's own daughters.

The questions about conventional male/female marriage and attitudes toward childlessness elicited intriguing replies from the respondents. Whereas a majority (58%) indicate that they have never been married to a man, 73% report they are childless. Of these, 64% feel positive about not having children.

Women surveyed had their first relationship (physical as well as emotional) with another female within a large age-range, some while still children and others after their 60th year (mean age being 25 years). These attachments have extended from one to 56 years' duration. Presently 42% are involved in a relationship with a woman.

More than half (53%) have had no physical/sexual encounter within the past year and more than a third label themselves "currently celibate," but three-fourths of these admit this is not by choice. Those few who wanted to change their sex, entertained the idea only in their early youth. Relationships with women within ten years of their age, and the practice of monogamy are favored by most of the respondents. According to one statistic (Pearson's Product Correlation = .18), sex was found to be less important after the age of 60 than before 60 for the group sampled.

These lesbians are survivors, with 72% reporting excellent or good physical health and 82% good or excellent emotional health. The most common complaints expressed are arthritis and cardiovascular problems but the majority are not affected to a degree that inhibits their activities. The majority (60%) reported that a partner or friend would take care of them when sick and they would visit a mental health professional, religious counselor or physician (72%) for help with emotional problems (Tables 20, 21). Drinking is not a serious problem (75% do not drink) with only 10% identifying as alcoholics, having been in recovery programs. Two-thirds do not smoke and the majority (58%) report that they exercise daily. The largest number (84%) feel positive about being lesbian and more than half (51%) feel the same about aging.

For the women who have felt discriminated against because of their lesbianism (28%), the circumstances more often centered around employment. Age discrimination, expressed by 34% of the sample, was most often felt in social situations with younger people and in the area of employment.

The composite person who emerges from this survey is a reasonably well-adjusted, happy individual who, in spite of the strain of living as a deviant, has been a productive citizen, functioning in what must have been, at least at times, an unsympathetic environment. Many of the comments attached to the questionnaire are revealing and appropriate as a conclusion to this report.

My years (approximately 20) as a closeted woman-identified-woman have been my strongest and most satisfying.

While I have always been comfortable with my lesbianism, the emotional strain of leading a double life has been severe. Only in very recent years, since retirement, and living in the unusually tolerant atmosphere that exists in the Bay Area, have I been able to relax somewhat and worry less about what society and my remaining family think of me.

Never regretted being a lesbian.

Now we are 79 and 80 sitting together in our living room . . . No one else knows about us.

I regret that I have not been able to discuss my lesbianism with my family.

My life experience as a lesbian has always been in conflict with my church membership. The need to lie in the world about the most important part of my life has always been painful.

Until I retired there was always the fear of being found out and fired. The gay revolution of the 70s brought more peace of mind.

I wouldn't trade my life experiences with anyone else.

The fact that my four children and I all relate to the same sex partners and that their father has, although married, homosexual tendencies puzzles me as to nature/nurture.

I wonder if finding someone isn't one of the biggest problems for older lesbians who are not in large cities.

I would very much like to join up with either a lesbian retirement community, or with a stable lesbian or women's community which would accept older women.

I fell in love for the first time when I was three. She was a few months younger.

I was involved in a sexual/emotional relationship with a woman when I was 40 years old. Did not consider myself lesbian. Much later, at age 69, I became interested in lesbian relationships and came out at 72 — after falling in love with a younger woman.

When I was very young, I never felt that I belonged.

It is hell when you lose the one person with whom you shared your life. We had no friends other than straight people — so since her death I have been unable to talk plainly to anyone.

When my youngest left home, I "came out." I've been a lesbian for the last 14 years.

My relationships with women were always like a solid marriage.

The loneliness that stems from being in the closet is almost unbearable.

We need a gay correspondence club and a women's bath house to break this wall of loneliness.

Like any minority—Women, Black, Asian, Hispanic—I think we all have a right to dignity and respect.

At this point in my life, I don't think of myself as a lesbian. I am a person who loves/feels affectionate in a non-sexual way. The fire hasn't gone out, but it's unlikely that sex can be a very large part of my life.

TABLES

Table 1

Age ranges	Relative frequencies (%)
60-64	44
65-69	32
70-74	13
75-86	9
*Unknown	2
Total	100

Table 2

Current place of residence	Relative frequencies (%)
Pacific Coast	54
Midwest	14
South	9
Mid Atlantic	9
Northeast	7
Rocky Mountains	3
Southwest	3
Unknown	1
Total	100

(*NOTE: If 2 responses were indicated, the answer was coded as "Unknown.")

Table 3

Setting reared	Relative frequencies (%)
Urban	44
Rural	21
Suburban	16
Small town	8
Unknown	11
Total	100

Table 4

Level of Education	Relative frequencies (%)
Graduate school	47
Four years college	20
Two years college	16
High school	13
Other	4
Total	100

Table 5

Type of housing	Relative frequencies (%)
Single dwelling/house	61
Apartment	25
Mobile home	3
Other	9
Unknown	2
Total	100

Table 6

Property status	Relative frequencies (%)
Owners	64
Renters	30
Unknown	6
Total	100

Table 7

Racial/ethnic identity	Relative frequencies (%)
White	93
Asian	2
American Indian	1
Black	1
Other	2
Unknown	1
Total	100

Table 8

Gross Income (1983)	Relative frequencies (%)
More than $50,000	4
$25,000-49,000	31
$15,000-24,999	25
$10,000-14,999	20
$5,000-9,999	14
Less than $5,000	3
Unknown	3
Total	100

Table 9

Political party affiliation	Relative frequencies (%)
Democratic	76
Republican	14
Independent	7
Other	3
Total	100

Table 10

Current religious identification	Relative frequencies (%)
Protestant	29
Catholic	13
Jewish	12
None	29
Other	16
Unknown	1
Total	100

Table 11

Occupation (when employed)	Relative frequencies (%)
Professional	70
Business	10
Clerical	8
Trades	4
Domestic	3
Land	1
Unknown	4
Total	100

Table 12

Sexual history	Relative frequencies (%)
Entirely homosexual	37
Largely homosexual with heterosexual	33
Largely heterosexual with homosexual	19
Equally heterosexual and homosexual	5
Entirely heterosexual	0
Without heterosexual or homosexual	1
Unknown	5
Total	100

Table 13

Sexual orientation of most friends	Relative frequencies (%)
Homosexual women (lesbians)	54
Heterosexual women	27
Homosexual men	2
Heterosexual men	0
Other	6
Unknown	11
Total	100

Table 14

Age of most lesbian friends	Relative frequencies (%)
More than 10 years younger	48
Within 10 years of my age	41
No lesbian friends	2
Other	3
Unknown	6
Total	100

Table 15

Where do you meet other lesbians?	Absolute frequency**
Community/social groups	71
Through friends	68
School/work	14
At bars	7

Table 16

How do you feel about --?	Mean Score***
Lesbian-only retirement community	2.3
Lesbian-only nursing home	2.5
Social organization for older lesbians	1.8
Lesbian/gay retirement community	3.9
Lesbian/gay nursing home	3.1
Social organization for older lesbians and gay men	2.6

Table 17

How often do you have contact with --?	Relative frequencies (%)			
	Once/mo+	Few times/year	Never+	Unknown
Mother	11	1	82	6
Sister	23	17	55	5
Daughter	17	6	72	5
Father	3	1	90	6
Brother	22	23	48	7
Son	9	7	78	6
Husband (or Ex)	4	5	84	7

Totals = 100%

+<u>Never</u> means don't have contact or deceased

(**NOTE: These are actual numbers, not percentages. More than one answer was permitted for this question.)

(***1=very positive; 2=somewhat positive; 3=neutral; 4=somewhat negative; 5=very negative)

Table 18

Where did you fit in family birth order?	Relative frequencies (%)
Eldest	31
Youngest	28
Middle	18
Only	11
Other	8
Unknown	4
Total	100

Table 19

People who know you are a lesbian	Mean Score****
Friends	1.5
Family	2.0

Table 20

Who would take care of you if sick?	Absolute frequencies
Partner/friend/neighbor	59
Family member	34
Professional or social health agency	21
Don't know	29

Table 21

Where would you go for emotional problems?	Absolute frequencies
Mental health professional, religious counselor, doctor	71
Lover/partner/friend	52
Family member	15
Don't know	2

(****1=most;2=some;3=none)

LESBIANS · OVER · 60:

A NATIONAL SURVEY

FOR

OLDER WOMEN WHOSE EMOTIONAL AND/OR SEXUAL

PREFERENCES ARE FOR OTHER WOMEN

PLEASE READ OUR LETTER ON PAGE 1 AND RESPOND TO ALL ITEMS WHICH ARE PRINTED ON BOTH SIDES OF EACH PAGE. FEEL FREE TO MAKE FURTHER COMMENTS IN THE MARGINS, ON THE LAST PAGE OF THE QUESTIONNAIRE, OR ON ADDITIONAL SHEETS. ALL COMMENTS WILL BE READ AND TAKEN INTO ACCOUNT.

THANK YOU FOR PARTICIPATING IN THIS SURVEY.

CENTER FOR RESEARCH AND EDUCATION IN SEXUALITY
SAN FRANCISCO STATE UNIVERSITY
SAN FRANCISCO, CALIFORNIA 94132

SPONSORED BY:

CHICAGO RESOURCE CENTER AND
GOLDEN GATE BUSINESS ASSOCIATION

CERES • *Center for Research and Education in Sexuality*

San Francisco State University

Psychology Building Room 502 • (415) 469-1137
1600 Holloway Avenue • San Francisco, California 94132

LESBIANS-OVER-60: A NATIONAL SURVEY

John P. DeCecco, Ph.D., *Project Director*
Monika Kehoe, Ph.D., *Project Coordinator*
Sheryl Goldberg, MSW, *Research Coordinator*

DEAR FRIEND:

FIRST, LET US INTRODUCE OURSELVES. WE ARE A TEAM MADE UP OF TWO LESBIANS, ONE A 74-YEAR-OLD AND THE OTHER AN "AGING" 28 YEAR-OLD. WE ARE CONDUCTING A NATION-WIDE PROJECT TO GATHER INFORMATION ON THE LIFE EXPERIENCES, THE STRENGTHS AS WELL AS NEEDS OF LESBIANS OVER 60. WE HOPE TO LEARN MORE ABOUT INDIVIDUAL ATTITUDES, BELIEFS, BEHAVIORS AND CHARACTERISTICS, SEEING WHAT SIMILARITIES AND DIFFERENCES EXIST.

THE INFORMATION YOU PROVIDE WILL HELP US TO COMPILE ONE OF THE FIRST COMPREHENSIVE REPORTS ON OLDER LESBIANS IN AMERICA. ALL INFORMATION YOU GIVE IS STRICTLY CONFIDENTIAL AND ANONYMOUS. THIS QUESTIONNAIRE MAY BE COMPLETED BY ANY LESBIAN AGED 60 AND OVER WHO FREELY CONSENTS TO ANSWER. THERE IS NO OBLIGATION TO PARTICIPATE AND NO FINANCIAL REWARD. SINCE WE ARE TRYING TO REACH AS MANY OLDER LESBIANS AS POSSIBLE, FEEL FREE TO WRITE AND REQUEST ADDITIONAL COPIES FOR YOU TO DISTRIBUTE TO OTHERS.

THE OVERALL RESULTS OF THIS SURVEY WILL BE MADE AVAILABLE TO ORGANIZATIONS AND AGENCIES WITHIN THE LESBIAN, GAY, AND ELDERLY SERVICE COMMUNITIES NATION-WIDE. YOU MAY RECEIVE A SUMMARY OF THE RESULTS BY WRITING "COPY OF RESULTS REQUESTED" ON THE BACK OF THE RETURN ENVELOPE AND PRINTING YOUR NAME AND ADDRESS BELOW IT. PLEASE DO NOT PUT THIS INFORMATION ON THE QUESTIONNAIRE ITSELF, SO THAT ANONYMITY MAY BE ASSURED.

WE WOULD BE HAPPY TO ANSWER ANY QUESTIONS YOU MIGHT HAVE. PLEASE FEEL FREE TO WRITE OR CALL.

THANK YOU VERY MUCH FOR YOUR TIME AND INFORMATION. WE APPRECIATE YOUR JOINING US IN OUR PROJECT.

SINCERELY,

MONIKA KEHOE, PH.D.
PROJECT COORDINATOR

SHERYL GOLDBERG, M.S.W.
RESEARCH COORDINATOR

LIFE-STYLE IDENTIFICATION

WE WOULD LIKE TO BEGIN BY ASKING ABOUT YOUR ATTITUDES
CONCERNING SOME WORDS AND EXPRESSIONS WHICH ARE USED TO IDENTIFY
THE LESBIAN LIFE-STYLE.

Q-1 HOW DO YOU <u>FEEL</u> ABOUT THE FOLLOWING WORDS AND EXPRESSIONS?
(PLEASE INDICATE WHETHER YOU FEEL VERY POSITIVE TO VERY
NEGATIVE ABOUT EACH ITEM BY CIRCLING THE APPROPRIATE NUMBER
FROM 1 TO 5)

		WHAT IS YOUR ATTITUDE? (CIRCLE NUMBER FOR EACH ITEM)				
		VERY POSITIVE	SOMEWHAT POSITIVE	NEUTRAL	SOMEWHAT NEGATIVE	VERY NEGATIVE
A	LESBIAN..........	1	2	3	4	5
B	GAY.............	1	2	3	4	5
C	HOMOSEXUAL.......	1	2	3	4	5
D	LESBIAN-FEMINIST.	1	2	3	4	5
E	LESBIAN-FEMINIST SEPARATIST.......	1	2	3	4	5
F	WOMAN-IDENTIFIED WOMAN...........	1	2	3	4	5
G	WOMEN-LOVING WOMEN...........	1	2	3	4	5
H	WOMEN WHO PREFER AND/OR LOVE WOMEN...........	1	2	3	4	5
I	WOMEN WHOSE EMOTIONAL/SEXUAL PREFERENCES ARE FOR OTHER WOMEN..	1	2	3	4	5
J	DYKE.............	1	2	3	4	5
K	BUTCH...........	1	2	3	4	5
L	FEMME...........	1	2	3	4	5
M	LOVER...........	1	2	3	4	5

Q-2 WHAT WORD DO YOU <u>PREFER</u> TO USE TO DESCRIBE YOUR EMOTIONAL
AND/OR SEXUAL PREFERENCE? (CIRCLE THE NUMBER OF YOUR ANSWER)

    1 LESBIAN
    2 GAY
    3 HOMOSEXUAL
    4 BISEXUAL
    5 OTHER (SPECIFY)_____

SOCIAL LIFE

WE WOULD LIKE TO KNOW HOW YOU CHOOSE TO SPEND YOUR SOCIAL TIME.

Q-3   WHAT IS/ARE YOUR PREFERRED FORM(S) OF RECREATION? (CIRCLE NUMBER(S) OF ALL THAT APPLY)

     1   ACTIVE SPORTS
     2   SPECTATOR SPORTS
     3   TELEVISION
     4   RADIO
     5   MOVIES
     6   CONCERTS AND/OR THEATER
     7   GARDENING
     8   TRAVELING
     9   READING
     10 OTHER (SPECIFY)_____

Q-4   WHICH WOMEN'S OR LESBIAN-IDENTIFIED PUBLICATIONS OR FORMS OF ENTERTAINMENT DO YOU PREFER? (CIRCLE NUMBER(S) OF ALL THAT APPLY)

     1   NEWSPAPERS
     2   MAGAZINES
     3   NEWSLETTERS
     4   BOOKS
     5   MUSIC
     6   FILMS
     7   NONE OF THE ABOVE
     8   OTHER (SPECIFY)_____

Q-5   ON THE AVERAGE, HOW OFTEN DO YOU SPEAK WITH OR SEE YOUR CLOSEST FRIENDS? (CIRCLE NUMBER)

     1   ONCE A DAY OR MORE
     2   ONE TO TWO TIMES A WEEK
     3   ONE TO TWO TIMES A MONTH
     4   A FEW TIMES A YEAR
     5   OTHER (SPECIFY)_____

Q-6   WHAT IS THE SEXUAL ORIENTATION OF MOST OF YOUR CLOSEST FRIENDS? (CIRCLE ONE NUMBER ONLY)

     1   LESBIAN
     2   GAY MEN
     3   HETEROSEXUAL WOMEN
     4   HETEROSEXUAL MEN
     5   OTHER (SPECIFY)_____

Q-7   WHAT ARE THE AGES OF MOST OF YOUR CLOSEST LESBIAN FRIENDS? (CIRCLE NUMBER)

     1   MORE THAN TEN YEARS YOUNGER THAN MYSELF
     2   WITHIN TEN YEARS OF MY AGE
     3   MORE THAN TEN YEARS OLDER
     4   I HAVE NO LESBIAN FRIENDS
     5   OTHER (SPECIFY)_____

Q-8   WHERE DO YOU MEET OTHER LESBIANS? (CIRCLE NUMBER(S) OF ALL ANSWERS THAT APPLY)

     1   AT BARS
     2   IN SOCIAL GROUPS
     3   AT SCHOOL
     4   THROUGH FRIENDS
     5   AT WORK
     6   AT COMMUNITY CENTERS
     7   OTHER (SPECIFY)_____

Q-9   WHAT PEOPLE KNOW/KNEW YOU ARE A LESBIAN?

	WHO KNOWS/KNEW YOU ARE A LESBIAN? (CIRCLE NUMBER FOR EACH ITEM)		
	MOST	SOME	NONE
A FRIENDS.............	1	2	3
B FAMILY..............	1	2	3
C NEIGHBORS...........	1	2	3
D CO-WORKERS..........	1	2	3
E OTHER (SPECIFY) _____.....	1	2	3

Q-10   HOW OFTEN DO YOU FREQUENT EACH OF THE FOLLOWING? (LESBIAN/GAY IS DEFINED AS A MIXED GROUP OF LESBIANS AND GAY MEN)

REGULARLY <u>MEANS</u> ABOUT ONCE A WEEK
OCCASIONALLY <u>MEANS</u> ABOUT ONCE A MONTH
SELDOM <u>MEANS</u> A FEW TIMES A YEAR
NEVER <u>MEANS</u> DON'T ATTEND BUT AWARE OF ORGANIZATION
UNAWARE <u>MEANS</u> DON'T KNOW ANY

	HOW OFTEN DO YOU FREQUENT? (CIRCLE NUMBER FOR EACH ITEM)				
	REGULARLY	OCCASIONALLY	SELDOM	NEVER	UNAWARE
A LESBIAN <u>ONLY</u> BARS.....	1	2	3	4	5
B LESBIAN/GAY BARS......	1	2	3	4	5
C LESBIAN <u>ONLY</u> SOCIAL GROUPS..........	1	2	3	4	5
D LESBIAN/GAY SOCIAL GROUPS................	1	2	3	4	5
E LESBIAN/GAY SOCIAL SERVICE ORGANIZATIONS..	1	2	3	4	5
F LESBIAN/GAY POLITICAL ORGANIZATIONS..........	1	2	3	4	5
G LESBIAN/GAY RELIGIOUS ORGANIZATIONS.:........	1	2	3	4	5

Q-11   DO YOU BELONG TO ANY LESBIAN-ONLY OR LESBIAN/GAY GROUPS? (CIRCLE NUMBER)

┌──1   YES
│   2   NO
↓

(IF YES)
Q-11A. PLEASE SPECIFY WHICH GROUPS.

_____

_____

_____

_____

SERVICES FOR OLDER ADULTS

THE NEXT SET OF QUESTIONS HAS TO DO WITH VARIOUS PROGRAMS AND
SERVICES DESIGNED FOR OLDER ADULTS. WE WOULD LIKE TO ASK ABOUT
YOUR PARTICIPATION IN SUCH PROGRAMS.

Q-12   HOW OFTEN DO YOU PARTICIPATE IN EACH OF THE PROGRAMS AND/OR USE
        THE SERVICES WHICH ARE LISTED BELOW?

          REGULARLY MEANS ABOUT ONCE A WEEK
       OCCASIONALLY MEANS ABOUT ONCE A MONTH
             SELDOM MEANS A FEW TIMES A YEAR
              NEVER MEANS DON'T PARTICIPATE BUT AWARE OF PROGRAM/SERVICE
            UNAWARE MEANS DON'T KNOW OF PROGRAM/SERVICE

HOW OFTEN DO YOU PARTICIPATE?
(CIRCLE NUMBER FOR EACH ITEM)

		REGULARLY	OCCASIONALLY	SELDOM	NEVER	UNAWARE
A	SENIOR CENTER PROGRAMS........	1	2	3	4	5
B	LESBIAN/GAY SENIOR SERVICE....	1	2	3	4	5
C	LEGAL SERVICES.....	1	2	3	4	5
D	HOME DELIVERED MEALS..........	1	2	3	4	5
E	NUTRITION CENTER...	1	2	3	4	5
F	HEALTH SERVICES....	1	2	3	4	5
G	IN-HOME HEALTH SERVICES.......	1	2	3	4	5
H	HOMEMAKER SERVICE..	1	2	3	4	5
I	TRANSPORTATION SERVICE........	1	2	3	4	5
J	MENTAL HEALTH COUNSELING......	1	2	3	4	5
K	OTHER (SPECIFY) _____	1	2	3	4	5

Q-13   WHERE DO YOU USUALLY HEAR ABOUT SUCH PROGRAMS AND SERVICES?
        (CIRCLE NUMBER(S) OF ALL THAT APPLY)

        1   TELEVISION AND/OR RADIO
        2   NEWSPAPERS
        3   SENIOR CENTER
        4   FRIENDS
        5   FAMILY
        6   PROFESSIONAL ORGANIZATIONS
        7   RELIGIOUS ORGANIZATIONS
        8   NOT AWARE OF ANY SERVICES
        9   OTHER (SPECIFY)_____

Q-14 How would/do you feel about living in each of the following?

		WHAT IS YOUR ATTITUDE? (CIRCLE NUMBER FOR EACH ITEM)				
		VERY POSITIVE	SOMEWHAT POSITIVE	NEUTRAL	SOMEWHAT NEGATIVE	VERY NEGATIVE
A	Lesbian Only Retirement Community...............	1	2	3	4	5
B	Lesbian/Gay Retirement Community...............	1	2	3	4	5
C	Women Only Retirement Community...............	1	2	3	4	5
D	Heterosexual Retirement Community...............	1	2	3	4	5
E	Lesbian Only Nursing Home....................	1	2	3	4	5
F	Lesbian/Gay Nursing Home....................	1	2	3	4	5
G	Women Only Nursing Home....................	1	2	3	4	5
H	Heterosexual Nursing Home....................	1	2	3	4	5

Q-15 How would/do you feel about participating in each of the following?

		WHAT IS YOUR ATTITUDE? (CIRCLE NUMBER FOR EACH ITEM)				
		VERY POSITIVE	SOMEWHAT POSITIVE	NEUTRAL	SOMEWHAT NEGATIVE	VERY NEGATIVE
A	Social Organization For Older Lesbians Only..................	1	2	3	4	5
B	Social Organization For Older Lesbians/ Gays.................	1	2	3	4	
C	Social Organization For Older Women.......	1	2	3	4	5
D	Social Organization for Older Women/Men...	1	2	3	4	5

Q-16 Below is a list of areas that can be problems for older adults. Please indicate which are problems for YOU TODAY. (Circle number(s) of all that apply)

1 INCOME
2 HOUSING
3 HEALTH CARE
4 TRANSPORTATION
5 EMPLOYMENT
6 AGE DISCRIMINATION
7 USE OF FREE TIME
8 CRIME
9 LONELINESS
10 NUTRITION
11 OTHER (Specify)_____

Q-17   WHICH OF THE ABOVE ARE THE MOST SERIOUS FOR YOU TODAY? (PUT
        THE NUMBER OF THE ITEM FROM THE ABOVE LIST ON THE APPROPRIATE
        LINE. IF NO ITEM IS A PROBLEM, PUT 0 ON THE LINE)

        _____ MOST SERIOUS PROBLEM

        _____ SECOND MOST SERIOUS PROBLEM

        _____ THIRD MOST SERIOUS PROBLEM

FAMILY RELATIONSHIPS

ONE IMPORTANT PURPOSE OF THIS STUDY IS TO LEARN ABOUT
YOUR PERSONAL RELATIONSHIPS. FIRST, WE WOULD LIKE TO ASK
ABOUT RELATIONSHIPS WITH MEMBERS OF YOUR IMMEDIATE OR
BIOLOGICAL FAMILY.

Q-18   PLEASE   INDICATE HOW OFTEN YOU ARE IN CONTACT WITH EACH OF
        THE FAMILY MEMBERS LISTED BELOW. IF THERE IS MORE THAN ONE
        PERSON IN THE SAME CATEGORY, ANSWER ABOUT THE PERSON YOU SEE
        MOST FREQUENTLY.

                REGULARLY MEANS ABOUT ONCE A WEEK
             OCCASIONALLY MEANS ABOUT ONCE A MONTH
                   SELDOM MEANS A FEW TIMES A YEAR
                    NEVER MEANS DON'T HAVE CONTACT WITH THIS PERSON
           DOES NOT APPLY MEANS NO SUCH PERSON OR DECEASED

HOW OFTEN DO YOU HAVE CONTACT?
(CIRCLE NUMBER FOR EACH ITEM)

		REGULARLY	OCCASIONALLY	SELDOM	NEVER	DOES NOT APPLY
A	MOTHER............	1	2	3	4	5
B	FATHER...........	1	2	3	4	5
C	SISTER...........	1	2	3	4	5
D	BROTHER..........	1	2	3	4	5
E	HUSBAND (OR EX):	1	2	3	4	5
F	DAUGHTER.........	1	2	3	4	5
G	SON..............	1	2	3	4	5
H	GRANDDAUGHTER....	1	2	3	4	5
I	GRANDSON.........	1	2	3	4	5
J	OTHER (SPECIFY) _____....	1	2	3	4	5

Q-19   WHERE DID YOU FIT IN THE BIRTH-ORDER OF YOUR FAMILY?
        (CIRCLE NUMBER)

        1   ELDEST CHILD
        2   MIDDLE CHILD
        3   YOUNGEST CHILD
        4   OTHER (SPECIFY)_____

Q-20   HOW MANY SIBLINGS DO/DID YOU HAVE? (FILL· IN BLANKS(S))

_____ SISTER(S)   _____ BROTHER(S)
(NUMBER)   (NUMBER)

Q-21   HAVE YOU EVER BEEN MARRIED TO A MAN? (CIRCLE NUMBER)

1   YES
2   NO

(IF YES)
Q-21A. HOW LONG DID THE MARRIAGE(S) LAST? (FILL IN BLANK(S))

1ST MARRIAGE _____ YEAR(S)
2ND MARRIAGE _____ YEAR(S)
3RD MARRIAGE _____ YEAR(S)

Q-22   HAVE YOU EVER HAD ANY CHILDREN? (CIRCLE NUMBER)

1   YES
2   NO

(IF YES)   (IF NO)
Q-22A. HOW MANY CHILDREN   Q-22B. HOW DO YOU FEEL ABOUT
HAVE YOU HAD? (FILL IN   NOT HAVING CHILDREN? (CIRCLE
BLANKS)   NUMBER)

_____ DAUGHTER(S)   1   VERY POSITIVE
(NUMBER)   2   SOMEWHAT POSITIVE
                                  3   NEUTRAL
_____ SON(S)   4   SOMEWHAT NEGATIVE
(NUMBER)   5   VERY NEGATIVE

Q-23   ARE ANY OTHER MEMBERS OF YOUR FAMILY LESBIAN OR GAY? (CIRCLE NUMBER)

1   YES
2   NO
3   DON'T KNOW

(IF YES)
Q-23A. SPECIFY WHICH MEMBERS (E.G. BROTHER, DAUGHTER, ETC.)

_____

_____

_____

_____

_____

Q-24   Do/did any members of your family know you are a lesbian?
(Circle number)

```
    ┌──1   YES
    │  2   NO────────┌─────────────────┐
    │                │  Go to Q-25     │
    ↓                └─────────────────┘
(If yes)
```

Q-24a. Fill in the blank with family member's relationship to
you (e.g. mother, son, etc.) and circle the number of the answer
which best describes her/his FEELINGS about your being a lesbian.

	WHAT IS THE ATTITUDE OF THIS PERSON? (Circle number for each item)					
Relationship(s)	VERY POSITIVE	SOMEWHAT POSITIVE	NEUTRAL	SOMEWHAT NEGATIVE	VERY NEGATIVE	DON'T KNOW
A _____	1	2	3	4	5	6
B _____	1	2	3	4	5	6
C _____	1	2	3	4	5	6
D _____	1	2	3	4	5	6

RELATIONSHIPS WITH WOMEN

Our next concern is learning about your relationships with other
women. For the following group of questions a RELATIONSHIP is
defined as having both emotional and physical/sexual components.

Q-25   At what age did you first recognize your emotional and physical/
sexual attraction to women? _____YEARS OLD

Q-26   Have you ever been involved in a relationship with a woman?
(Circle number)

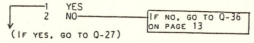

```
    ┌──1   YES
    │  2   NO────────┌─────────────────────────┐
    │                │  If no, go to Q-36      │
    ↓                │  on page 13             │
(If yes, go to Q-27) └─────────────────────────┘
```

Q-27   How old were you when you had your first relationship with another
woman? _____YEARS OLD

Q-28   Are you CURRENTLY involved in a relationship with a woman?
(Circle number)

```
    ┌──1   YES
    │  2   NO
    ↓
(If yes)
```
Q-28a. How long have you been in this relationship?
_____MONTH(S) and/or _____YEAR(S)

Q-29   What is the longest time you have spent in a relationship with
another woman? _____MONTH(S) and/or _____YEAR(S)

Q-30   What has been the greatest age difference between you and a
woman partner/lover? _____YEAR(S)

Q-30a. Were/are you: (Circle number)

     1   YOUNGER
     2   OLDER

Q-31 HAS A WOMAN PARTNER/LOVER OF YOURS EVER DIED WHILE YOU WERE TOGETHER ? (CIRCLE NUMBER)

   1   YES
   2   NO————————— IF NO, GO TO Q-32
                    ON PAGE 13

(IF YES)
Q-31A. WHAT WERE YOUR RESPECTIVE AGES AT THE TIME OF DEATH?
_____MY AGE   _____MY PARTNER'S AGE

Q-31B. AS A LESBIAN, DID YOU EXPERIENCE ANY ADDITIONAL CONCERNS (E.G. LEGAL, EMOTIONAL) IN DEALING WITH THIS DEATH? (CIRCLE NUMBER)

   1   YES
   2   NO

(IF YES)
Q-31C. PLEASE DESCRIBE THESE CONCERNS AND YOUR EXPERIENCE.

_____
_____
_____
_____
_____

Q-32 BEFORE AGE 60, WERE YOUR RELATIONSHIPS WITH WOMEN USUALLY WITH PARTNERS: (CIRCLE ONE NUMBER ONLY)

   1   MORE THAN TEN YEARS YOUNGER THAN MYSELF
   2   WITHIN TEN YEARS OF MY AGE
   3   MORE THAN TEN YEARS OLDER
   4   NO RELATIONSHIPS BEFORE AGE 60

Q-33 AFTER AGE 60, ARE YOUR RELATIONSHIPS WITH WOMEN USUALLY WITH PARTNERS: (CIRCLE ONE NUMBER ONLY)

   1   MORE THAN TEN YEARS YOUNGER THAN MYSELF
   2   WITHIN TEN YEARS OF MY AGE
   3   MORE THAN TEN YEARS OLDER
   4   NO RELATIONSHIPS AFTER AGE 60

Q-34 SINCE AGE 60, HAVE YOUR RELATIONSHIPS WITH WOMEN DIFFERED FROM THOSE YOU HAD BEFORE THEN? (CIRCLE NUMBER)

   1   YES
   2   NO

(IF YES)
Q-34A. SPECIFY IN WHAT WAYS YOUR RELATIONSHIPS ARE DIFFERENT NOW.

_____
_____
_____
_____

Q-35   HAVE THERE BEEN CONVENTIONAL HETEROSEXUAL ROLES PLAYED IN
       YOUR RELATIONSHIPS (E.G. HUSBAND-WIFE, BUTCH-FEMME)? (CIRCLE
       NUMBER)

       1   YES
       2   NO
       3   SOMETIMES

Q-36   DO YOU PREFER TO BE IN EMOTIONAL AND PHYSICAL/SEXUAL RELATIONSHIPS
       WITH WOMEN WHO ARE: (CIRCLE NUMBER)

       1   MORE THAN TEN YEARS YOUNGER THAN MYSELF
       2   WITHIN TEN YEARS OF MY AGE
       3   MORE THAN TEN YEARS OLDER
       4   NO PREFERENCE
       5   OTHER (SPECIFY)_____

SEXUALITY

THE NEXT SERIES OF QUESTIONS DEALS WITH YOUR SEXUAL ATTITUDES
AND ACTIVITIES.

Q-37   USING THE SCALE GIVEN BELOW, PLEASE RATE YOURSELF ON THE BASIS
       OF YOUR SEXUAL HISTORY. (CIRCLE THE NUMBER WHICH MOST CLOSELY
       DESCRIBES YOUR EXPERIENCE)
                                    EXCLUSIVELY
       1   ENTIRELY HETEROSEXUAL

       2   LARGELY HETEROSEXUAL BUT WITH INCIDENTAL
           HOMOSEXUAL HISTORY

       3   LARGELY HETEROSEXUAL BUT WITH DISTINCT
           HOMOSEXUAL HISTORY

       4   EQUALLY HETEROSEXUAL AND HOMOSEXUAL

       5   LARGELY HOMOSEXUAL BUT WITH DISTINCT
           HETEROSEXUAL HISTORY

       6   LARGELY HOMOSEXUAL BUT WITH INCIDENTAL
           HETEROSEXUAL HISTORY

       7   ENTIRELY HOMOSEXUAL

       8   WITHOUT EITHER HOMOSEXUAL OR HETEROSEXUAL
           HISTORY

Q-38   PLEASE INDICATE THE ONE CHOICE WHICH BEST DESCRIBES YOUR
       SEXUAL ORIENTATION AND FEELINGS WITHIN THE PAST TWO YEARS.

| | WHAT IS YOUR SEXUAL ORIENTATION? (CIRCLE NUMBER FOR EACH ITEM) | | | | | |
	WOMEN ONLY	USUALLY WOMEN	EQUALLY WOMEN & MEN	USUALLY MEN	MEN ONLY	NONE
A	WITH WHOM HAVE YOU HAD EMOTIONAL RELATIONSHIPS?......1	2	3	4	5	6
B	WITH WHOM HAVE YOU HAD PHYSICAL/ SEXUAL ACTIVITY?....1	2	3	4	5	6
C	ABOUT WHOM HAVE YOU HAD EROTIC FANTASIES?..........1	2	3	4	5	6

Q-39 DO YOU FEEL THAT BEING A LESBIAN IS YOUR CHOICE? (CIRCLE NUMBER)

    1 ENTIRELY MY CHOICE
    2 MOSTLY MY CHOICE
    3 PARTLY MY CHOICE
    4 NOT MY CHOICE AT ALL
    5 DON'T KNOW

Q-40 OVER THE LAST YEAR, HOW OFTEN WERE YOU PHYSICALLY SEXUAL WITH ANOTHER WOMAN? (CIRCLE NUMBER)

    1 DAILY
    2 ABOUT ONCE A WEEK
    3 ABOUT ONCE A MONTH
    4 A FEW TIMES A YEAR
    5 NEVER
    6 OTHER (SPECIFY)_____

Q-41 OVERALL, HOW SATISFIED HAVE YOU BEEN WITH YOUR SEX LIFE OVER THE LAST YEAR? (CIRCLE NUMBER)

    1 VERY SATISFIED
    2 SOMEWHAT SATISFIED
    3 NEITHER SATISFIED NOR UNSATISFIED
    4 SOMEWHAT UNSATISFIED
    5 VERY UNSATISFIED

Q-42 ARE YOU CURRENTLY CELIBATE? (CIRCLE NUMBER)

    1 YES
    2 NO————— IF NO, GO TO Q-43

(IF YES)
Q-42A. FOR HOW LONG HAVE YOU BEEN CELIBATE?

    _____MONTH(S) AND/OR _____YEAR(S)

Q-42B. IS CELIBACY YOUR CHOICE? (CIRCLE NUMBER)

    1 YES
    2 NO

Q-43 BEFORE AGE 60, HOW IMPORTANT WAS SEX TO YOU IN A LESBIAN RELATIONSHIP? (CIRCLE NUMBER)

    1 SEX WAS THE MAIN PART
    2 SEX WAS ONE IMPORTANT PART
    3 SEX WAS NOT AN IMPORTANT PART

Q-44 SINCE AGE 60, HOW IMPORTANT IS SEX TO YOU IN A LESBIAN RELATIONSHIP? (CIRCLE NUMBER)

    1 SEX IS THE MAIN PART
    2 SEX IS ONE IMPORTANT PART
    3 SEX IS AN UNIMPORTANT PART

Q-45 WHAT IS YOUR ATTITUDE ABOUT MONOGAMY IN LESBIAN RELATIONSHIPS? (CIRCLE NUMBER)

    1 VERY POSITIVE
    2 SOMEWHAT POSITIVE
    3 NEUTRAL
    4 SOMEWHAT NEGATIVE
    5 VERY NEGATIVE

Q-46 HAVE YOU EVER WANTED TO CHANGE YOUR SEX? (CIRCLE NUMBER)

```
      ┌──1   YES
      │   2   NO
      ↓
```

(IF YES)
Q-46A.   AT WHAT AGE(S) WAS/IS THIS TRUE FOR YOU?

_____YEARS OLD

HEALTH

THE FOLLOWING SET OF QUESTIONS DEALS WITH YOUR PHYSICAL AND EMOTIONAL HEALTH.

Q-47 HOW WOULD YOU DESCRIBE YOUR PHYSICAL HEALTH AT THE PRESENT TIME? (CIRCLE NUMBER OF YOUR ANSWER)

    1   EXCELLENT
    2   GOOD
    3   FAIR
    4   POOR
    5   OTHER (SPECIFY)_____

Q-48 FOR EACH OF THE FOLLOWING PHYSICAL CONDITIONS, PLEASE RATE YOURSELF.

	WHAT IS YOUR PHYSICAL CONDITION? (CIRCLE NUMBER FOR EACH ITEM)			
	EXCELLENT	GOOD	FAIR	POOR
A VISION - WITH GLASSES/CONTACTS.....	1	2	3	4
B HEARING - WITHOUT HEARING AID.........	1	2	3	4
C MOBILITY - WALKING WITHOUT ASSISTANCE...	1	2	3	4

Q-49 DO YOU PRESENTLY HAVE ANY PHYSICAL PROBLEM(S) OR ILLNESS(ES) THAT SERIOUSLY AFFECT(S) YOUR HEALTH OR RESTRICT(S) YOUR ACTIVITY? (CIRCLE NUMBER)

```
      ┌──1   YES
      │   2   NO
      ↓
```

(IF YES)
Q-49A. SPECIFY WHAT PHYSICAL PROBLEM(S) OR ILLNESS(ES).

_____

_____

_____

_____

Q-50   DO YOU TAKE ANY MEDICATIONS? (CIRCLE NUMBER)

    1   YES
    2   NO

(IF YES)
Q-50A. WHAT MEDICATION(S) DO YOU TAKE?

_____

_____

_____

Q-51   DO YOU DRINK ALCOHOLIC BEVERAGES--INCLUDING BEER, WINE AND LIQUOR?
(CIRCLE NUMBER)

    1   YES
    2   NO

(IF YES)
Q-51A. HOW OFTEN DO YOU DRINK ALCOHOLIC BEVERAGES?

    1   DAILY
    2   ABOUT ONCE A WEEK
    3   ABOUT ONCE A MONTH
    4   A FEW TIMES A YEAR
    5   OTHER (SPECIFY)_____

Q-51B. WHEN YOU DRINK ALCOHOLIC BEVERAGES, HOW MANY DRINKS DO
YOU <u>USUALLY</u> HAVE AT ONE TIME? (CIRCLE NUMBER)

    1   ONE
    2   TWO
    3   THREE OR MORE

Q-52   DO YOU CONSIDER YOURSELF TO BE AN ALCOHOLIC? (CIRCLE NUMBER)

    1   YES
    2   NO
    3   DON'T KNOW

Q-53   HAVE YOU BEEN OR ARE YOU A MEMBER OF. AN ALCOHOL RECOVERY PROGRAM?
(CIRCLE NUMBER)

    1   YES
    2   NO

Q-54   DO YOU SMOKE ANY OF THE FOLLOWING?   (CIRCLE NUMBER(S) OF ALL
THAT APPLY)

    1   CIGARETTES
    2   CIGAR
    3   PIPE
    4   MARIJUANA
    5   DON'T SMOKE

Q-55   DO YOU CONSIDER YOURSELF? (CIRCLE NUMBER)

    1   TOO FAT
    2   JUST RIGHT
    3   TOO THIN

Q-56   HOW OFTEN DO YOU EXERCISE (E.G. DO CALISTHENICS, TAKE A
        LONG WALK OR DO VIGOROUS GARDENING)? (CIRCLE NUMBER)

        1   DAILY
        2   ABOUT ONCE A WEEK
        3   ABOUT ONCE A MONTH
        4   A FEW TIMES A YEAR
        5   NEVER
        6   OTHER (SPECIFY)_____

Q-57   WHO WOULD HELP YOU OR TAKE CARE OF YOU IF YOU WERE VERY SICK
        OR DISABLED? (CIRCLE NUMBER(S) OF ALL THAT APPLY)

        1   PARTNER/LOVER
        2   FAMILY MEMBER
        3   FRIEND
        4   NEIGHBOR
        5   SOCIAL AND/OR HEALTH SERVICE AGENCY
        6   DON'T KNOW
        7   OTHER (SPECIFY)_____

Q-58   HOW WOULD YOU DESCRIBE YOUR <u>EMOTIONAL</u> HEALTH? (CIRCLE NUMBER)

        1   EXCELLENT
        2   GOOD
        3   FAIR
        4   POOR
        5   OTHER (SPECIFY)_____

Q-59   TO WHOM WOULD YOU GO TO SEEK HELP WITH EMOTIONAL HEALTH
        PROBLEMS? (CIRCLE NUMBER(S) OF ALL THAT APPLY)

        1   MENTAL HEALTH PROFESSIONAL (E.G. SOCIAL WORKER OR
             PSYCHOLOGIST)
        2   PHYSICIAN
        3   RELIGIOUS COUNSELOR
        4   PARTNER/LOVER
        5   FRIEND
        6   FAMILY MEMBER
        7   OTHER (SPECIFY)_____

Q-60   HERE ARE SOME STATEMENTS CONCERNING LIFE SATISFACTION. PLEASE
        INDICATE HOW YOU FEEL ABOUT EACH ONE.

		WHAT ARE YOUR FEELINGS? (CIRCLE NUMBER FOR EACH ITEM)		
		AGREE	DISAGREE	NOT SURE
A	I AM JUST AS HAPPY AS WHEN I WAS YOUNGER........	1	2	3
B	THESE ARE THE BEST YEARS OF MY LIFE..........	1	2	3
C	THIS IS THE DREARIEST TIME OF MY LIFE...........	1	2	3
D	MOST OF THE THINGS I DO ARE BORING OR MONOTONOUS..	1	2	3
E	COMPARED WITH OTHER PEOPLE, I GET DOWN IN THE DUMPS TOO OFTEN.................	1	2	3
F	THE THINGS I DO ARE AS INTERESTING TO ME AS THEY EVER WERE............	1	2	3

	AGREE	DISAGREE	NOT SURE
G I HAVE MADE PLANS FOR THINGS I'LL BE DOING A MONTH OR A YEAR FROM NOW..	1	2	3
H AS I GROW OLDER, THINGS SEEM BETTER THAN I THOUGHT THEY WOULD BE.....	1	2	3
I AS I LOOK BACK ON MY LIFE, I AM FAIRLY WELL SATISFIED...........	1	2	3
J I'VE GOTTEN PRETTY MUCH WHAT I EXPECTED OUT OF LIFE..............	1	2	3
K WHEN I THINK BACK OVER MY LIFE, I DIDN'T GET MOST OF THE IMPORTANT THINGS I WANTED..........	1	2	3
L IN SPITE OF WHAT PEOPLE SAY, THE LOT OF THE AVERAGE PERSON IS GETTING WORSE, NOT BETTER........	1	2	3
M I HAVE GOTTEN MORE OF THE BREAKS IN LIFE THAN MOST OF THE PEOPLE I KNOW......	1	2	3

Q-61   HAVE YOU EVER BEEN IN THERAPY CONCERNING YOUR LESBIANISM? (CIRCLE NUMBER)

```
┌───1   YES
│    2   NO
↓
```
(IF YES)
Q-61A.   ARE YOU <u>PRESENTLY</u> IN THERAPY FOR THIS SAME REASON?

    1   YES
    2   NO

Q-62   HOW DO YOU FEEL ABOUT BEING A LESBIAN?   (CIRCLE NUMBER)

    1   VERY POSITIVE
    2   SOMEWHAT POSITIVE
    3   NEUTRAL
    4   SOMEWHAT NEGATIVE
    5   VERY NEGATIVE

Q-63   HAVE YOU EVER FELT DISCRIMINATED AGAINST BECAUSE OF YOUR LESBIANISM?   (CIRCLE NUMBER)

```
┌───1   YES
│    2   NO
↓
```
(IF YES)
Q-63A.   PLEASE SPECIFY THE CIRCUMSTANCES.

_____

_____

_____

Q-64 HOW DO YOU FEEL ABOUT YOUR OWN AGING? (CIRCLE NUMBER)

      1 VERY POSITIVE
      2 SOMEWHAT POSITIVE
      3 NEUTRAL
      4 SOMEWHAT NEGATIVE
      5 VERY NEGATIVE

Q-65 HAVE YOU EVER FELT DISCRIMINATED AGAINST BECAUSE OF YOUR AGE? (CIRCLE NUMBER)

      1 YES
      2 NO

(IF YES)
Q-65A. PLEASE SPECIFY THE CIRCUMSTANCES.

_____

_____

_____

_____

_____

Q-66 HAVE YOU EVER FELT DISCRIMINATED AGAINST WITHIN THE LESBIAN COMMUNITY BECAUSE OF YOUR AGE? (CIRCLE NUMBER)

      1 YES
      2 NO

(IF YES)
Q-66A. PLEASE SPECIFY THE CIRCUMSTANCES.

_____

_____

_____

_____

_____

BACKGROUND INFORMATION

FINALLY, WE WOULD LIKE TO ASK SOME QUESTIONS ABOUT YOUR BACKGROUND AND PRESENT SITUATION.

Q-67 WHAT IS YOUR DATE OF BIRTH? _____
                                 MONTH/DAY/YEAR

Q-68 WHERE WERE YOU BORN?_____
                             TOWN OR CITY/STATE/COUNTRY

Q-69 IN WHAT KIND OF SETTING WERE YOU REARED? (CIRCLE NUMBER)

      1 RURAL
      2 URBAN
      3 SUBURBAN
      4 OTHER (SPECIFY)_____

Q-70 WHERE DO YOU LIVE NOW?_____
                             TOWN OR CITY/STATE/COUNTRY

Q-71 IN WHAT TYPE OF HOUSING DO YOU LIVE? (CIRCLE NUMBER)

1 SINGLE DWELLING/HOUSE
2 APARTMENT
3 MOBILE HOME
4 ROOMING HOUSE
5 BOARD-AND-CARE FACILITY
6 HOTEL
7 OTHER (SPECIFY)_____

Q-72 ARE YOU A: (CIRCLE NUMBER)

1 HOMEOWNER
2 RENTER

Q-73 WHAT IS YOUR <u>PRESENT</u> LIVING ARRANGEMENT? (CIRCLE NUMBER)

1 LIVE ALONE————————— IF #1, GO TO Q-74
2 SHARE HOUSING   ON PAGE 24
3 OTHER (SPECIFY)_____

(IF YOU SHARE HOUSING)
Q-73A. WITH WHOM DO YOU LIVE?

1 LOVER
2 FRIEND(S)
3 RELATIVE(S) (SPECIFY)_____
4 OTHER (SPECIFY)_____

Q-73B. FOR HOW LONG HAVE YOU LIVED TOGETHER?_____YEAR(S)

Q-74 WHAT IS YOUR <u>PRESENT</u> RELATIONSHIP STATUS? (CIRCLE ONE NUMBER ONLY)

1 IN A COMMMITTED RELATIONSHIP WITH A WOMAN

2 SEPARATED FROM A RELATIONSHIP WITH A WOMAN

3 WIDOWED FROM A RELATIONSHIP WITH A WOMAN

4 UNATTACHED: NOT IN A CURRENT RELATIONSHIP

5 IN A HETEROSEXUAL MARRIAGE

6 SEPARATED/DIVORCED FROM A HETEROSEXUAL MARRIAGE

7 WIDOWED FROM A HETEROSEXUAL MARRIAGE

8 OTHER (SPECIFY) _____

Q-75 WITH WHICH RACIAL/ETHNIC GROUP DO YOU IDENTIFY? (CIRCLE NUMBER)

1 AMERICAN INDIAN
2 ASIAN
3 BLACK
4 HISPANIC
5 WHITE
6 OTHER (SPECIFY)_____

Q-76 WITH WHICH RELIGIOUS OR SPIRITUAL GROUP DO YOU IDENTIFY? (CIRCLE NUMBER)

1 CATHOLIC
2 JEWISH
3 PROTESTANT (SPECIFY DENOMINATION)_____
4 BUDDHIST
5 NONE
6 OTHER (SPECIFY)_____

Q-77 HOW FREQUENTLY DO YOU ATTEND RELIGIOUS OR SPIRITUAL SERVICES? (CIRCLE NUMBER)

1 DAILY
2 ABOUT ONCE A WEEK
3 ABOUT ONCE A MONTH
4 A FEW TIMES A YEAR
5 NEVER
6 OTHER (SPECIFY)_____

Q-78 ARE YOU AN EX-NUN? (CIRCLE NUMBER)

1 YES
2 NO

(IF YES)
Q-78A. HOW OLD WERE YOU WHEN YOU LEFT YOUR COMMUNITY?
_____YEARS OLD

Q-79 IN WHICH POLITICAL PARTY ARE YOU <u>PRESENTLY</u> REGISTERED TO VOTE? (CIRCLE NUMBER)

1 DEMOCRATIC
2 INDEPENDENT
3 REPUBLICAN
4 NOT REGISTERED TO VOTE
5 OTHER (SPECIFY)_____

Q-80 WHAT IS YOUR <u>HIGHEST</u> LEVEL OF EDUCATION? (CIRCLE ONE NUMBER ONLY)

1 NO FORMAL EDUCATION
2 GRADE SCHOOL
3 HIGH SCHOOL
4 TWO YEARS OF COLLEGE
5 FOUR-YEAR COLLEGE (SPECIFY DEGREE(S))_____
6 GRADUATE SCHOOL (SPECIFY DEGREE(S))_____
7 OTHER (SPECIFY)_____

Q-81 DO YOU CURRENTLY ATTEND COLLEGE OR CLASSES IN CONTINUING EDUCATION? (CIRCLE NUMBER)

1 YES
2 NO

(IF YES)
Q-81A. SPECIFY WHICH COURSE(S)_____

_____

Q-82 DID YOU SERVE IN THE MILITARY? (CIRCLE NUMBER)

1 YES
2 NO

(IF YES)
Q-82A. DID YOU RECEIVE A DISCHARGE BECAUSE OF YOUR LESBIANISM? (CIRCLE NUMBER)

1 YES
2 NO

Q-83 ARE YOU CURRENTLY: (CIRCLE NUMBER)

1 EMPLOYED, FULL TIME
2 EMPLOYED, PART TIME
3 NOT EMPLOYED, SEEKING WORK
4 NOT EMPLOYED, <u>NOT</u> SEEKING WORK
5 RETIRED

Q-84 WHAT IS YOUR <u>USUAL</u> OCCUPATION WHEN EMPLOYED (OR BEFORE RETIREMENT)? (FILL IN BLANKS)

    A JOB TITLE_____
    B KIND OF WORK_____

        _____

        _____

    C KIND OF AGENCY, BUSINESS OR COMPANY_____

        _____

        _____

Q-85 WHICH OF THESE BROAD CATEGORIES BEST DESCRIBES <u>YOUR GROSS</u> INCOME IN 1983 (BEFORE TAXES AND OTHER DEDUCTIONS) (CIRCLE NUMBER)

    1   LESS THAN $5,000
    2   $5,000 TO $9,999
    3   $10,000 TO $14,999
    4   $15,000 TO $24,999
    5   $25,000 TO $49,999
    6   MORE THAN $50,000

Q-86 HOW DID YOU LEARN ABOUT THIS STUDY?_____

_____

_____

Q-87 WHAT COMMENTS, IF ANY, DO YOU HAVE ABOUT THE ITEMS WITHIN THIS QUESTIONNAIRE?

_____

_____

_____

IF THERE IS ANYTHING ELSE YOU WOULD LIKE TO TELL US ABOUT YOUR LIFE EXPERIENCE AS A LESBIAN, PLEASE FEEL FREE TO USE THE SPACE BELOW.

YOUR CONTRIBUTION TO THIS EFFORT IS GREATLY APPRECIATED. ALL OF YOUR RESPONSES WILL BE HELD IN THE STRICTEST CONFIDENCE. IF YOU WOULD LIKE ADDITIONAL COPIES OF THIS QUESTIONNAIRE AND/OR A SUMMARY OF THE RESULTS, PRINT YOUR NAME AND ADDRESS ON THE BACK OF THE RETURN ENVELOPE (<u>NOT</u> ON THIS QUESTIONNAIRE) AND INDICATE YOUR SPECIFIC REQUEST. WE THANK YOU AGAIN FOR YOUR PARTICIPATION IN THIS SURVEY.